She Changed Comics

The Untold Story of the Women Who Changed Free Expression in Comics

Presented by
Comic Book Legal Defense Fund

Edited by
Betsy Gomez

Contributors
Maren Williams
Caitlin McCabe
Casey Gilly
Charles Brownstein
Frenchy Lunning
Lauren Bullock

She Changed Comics: The Untold Story of the Women Who Changed Free Expression in Comics

Book layout by Betsy Gomez.

Copyedited by Charles Howitt and Julie Patterson.

Cover design by Sasha Head.

Cover art: Miss Fury by Tarpé Mills. Excerpted from strip originally published March 21, 1943. Courtesy the Library of American Comics / IDW Publishing.

Kickstarter fundraising logo designed by Joyana McDiarmid.

Published by Image Comics. Inc.
2001 Center St., Sixth Floor
Berkeley, CA 94704

First edition: October 2016
ISBN 978-1-63215-929-8

10 9 8 7 6 5 4 3 2 1
Printed in the United States of America.
For more information regarding the CPSIA on this printed material call: 203-595-3636 and provide reference # RICH - 706731.

For international rights, please contact: foreignlicensing@imagecomics.com

CORPORATE MEMBERS

CONTENTS

EDITOR'S NOTE

Women's contributions to free expression in the comics medium have been overlooked for way too long, so we wanted to tell their story.

The idea that women don't read and don't make comics was wrong before it was ever uttered aloud. Women have been making comics since their inception, and there was even something resembling gender parity in readership prior to the implementation of the Comics Code in 1954. But as the mainstream comics industry focused increasingly on superhero comics—a genre that appealed mainly to boys—to survive the Code, many women had to find other spaces in which to express themselves. They turned to underground comix, alternative comics, and webcomics. Today, after a long period of near-erasure, women comics creators are dominating the mainstream and *The New York Times* bestseller lists, they're increasing the diversity of the medium, and readership is once again approaching parity. This is possible because of the women who came before.

How did we go about selecting the women featured in this book? The first part was easy: we started with the women who had been challenged and banned—women whose work posed such a dire threat to the personal beliefs of some individuals that they demanded the books and art be removed from galleries, libraries, schools, and bookstores. Then, we looked at the work of women who were first in their fields and who held the door open for the women who followed. Finally, we focused on the work of women whose contributions to free expression in the medium moved the line, taking what comics could say in new directions and into new spaces.

Did we get it right? I like to think so, but that's where you come in: if we overlooked someone, then tell her story! The more stories we tell about the

She CHANGED COMICS

Fundraising logo designed by Joyana McDiarmid.

women who changed free expression in comics, the less women's contributions can be disregarded.

She Changed Comics is a starting point. Our hope is that this book inspires its readers to explore further. Comics wouldn't be the same without the contributions of the women profiled here, and they laid the groundwork for what's to come!

—*Betsy Gomez, August 2016*

Special Thanks

There are so many people who made this project possible, not least of them the contributors listed at the end of this book, who generously gave to our Kickstarter campaign in support of the book. The response was phenomenal, thank you!

The extraordinary support of the Gaiman Foundation makes our education program possible. Thank you.

We would like to thank the publishers who generously assisted in obtaining images for the book: Abrams, BOOM!, Dark Horse Comics, DC Comics, Drawn & Quarterly, Dynamite Entertainment, Fantagraphics, First Second, Groundwood Books, HarperCollins, Houghton Mifflin Harcourt, IDW and The Library of American Comics, Image Comics, Koyama, Last Gasp, Marvel, North Atlantic Books, Pantheon, Scholastic, Top Shelf, and VIZ Media. Thanks also to Kate Beaton, Barbara Brandon-Croft, Sophie Campbell, Sue Coe and Fay Duftler, Colleen Doran, Nancy Goldstein, Carol Lay, Kate Leth, Lee Marrs and Justin Hall, Lena Merhej, Françoise Mouly, Wendy and Richard Pini, C. Spike Trotman, and the Billy Ireland Cartoon Library and Museum.

We are grateful for the outstanding support provided by the team at Image Comics in helping us take this book into the world.

A sincere thanks to Trina Robbins, whose historical publications about women in comics proved invaluable during the research and writing phases of *She Changed Comics*.

Finally, we would like to thank the women who changed free expression: the women profiled in this book and the women who volunteered their time to be interviewed for it. These women inspired the generations that followed, the generations to come, and us!

Kathleen and the Great Secret
By Nell Brinkley

The American Weekly
Section of the San Francisco Examiner, Sunday, December 26, 1920
Copyright, 1920, by International Feature Service, Inc.   Great Britain Rights Reserved.

Nell Brinkley's "Kathleen and the Great Secret" ran over 18 weeks in 1920–1921.
(Published in *The American Weekly* December 26, 1920. Courtesy Fantagraphics.)

NELL BRINKLEY
Golden Age • Illustrator

Often credited as the "Queen of Comics" during her time, Nell Brinkley was one of the pioneering women who helped shape the fledgling comics industry at the turn of the 20th century. With her innovative and unique style and her fresh young voice, she would also usher in a new era for women both on and off the page, enabling them to openly and freely express themselves.

Born in Denver in 1886, Nell Brinkley had a professional career that spanned almost four decades and included illustration work in some of the most popular publications of the time, such as *The Evening Journal, Harper's Magazine*, and *The American Weekly*. She was also the creator of original comic strips like *The Fortunes of Flossie, Romances of Gloriette*, and *The Adventures of Prudence Prim*, all of which depicted the fantastic one-page adventures of women protagonists. In a time when women illustrators were few and far between, Brinkley created works and characters that spoke to and fueled an American public growing into its new century.

It was her most iconic and lasting creation, the "Brinkley Girl," a working girl with bouncy curls, an organic disposition, and a careless, whimsical air, that would inspire generations of young women and comics creators for years to come. Along with becoming a national symbol synonymous with the Roaring '20s, the enormously popular Brinkley Girl would also become a national icon that would influence high fashion, entertainment, and pop culture and inspire expression in other media, from film to music.

What made Brinkley a unique and sometimes contentious figure in the early 1900s was the strong sense of ambition that imbued her works and characters. Even at the tender age of 20, Brinkley spoke of the possibilities of freedom for women both on the editorial page and in society at large. Brinkley often found the opportunity to use her work to promote the roles of working women and the expansion of women's rights, including suffrage. In a time when the women's suffrage movement was in full force, Brinkley's work instilled women with a sense of pride and confidence. It would be Brinkley's combination of mystique, self-assurance, and poise, coupled with her fine line style, that would inspire future pioneering women comics creators, including Dale Messick, the creator of the popular 1940s comic *Brenda Starr*, who credited Brinkley as one of her greatest influences.

Despite her incredible popularity, some critiqued the strange and atypical characters that Brinkley created—what we would recognize and celebrate today as strong female characters. Brinkley kept on creating, seemingly unfazed by the criticism and controversy. Furthermore, even if one person wrote a letter to their local paper asking if there was "any good reason why a woman's head should be portrayed as weather-beaten moss instead of human hair" (Robbins 2013), many rose to her defense. In response to the criticism, *The Los Angeles Examiner* compared Brinkley's work to that of Botticelli, Da Vinci, Raphael, Michelangelo, and other classic artists. The *Examiner* also defended and immortalized Brinkley's influence in verse:

The sweetest, neatest, fleetest maid—the leader in her class,

Give me the stylish, smilish, wilish, dashing Brinkley Lass. (Robbins 2013)

FURTHER READING

The Brinkley Girls: The Best of Nell Brinkley's Cartoons from 1913–1940 by Trina Robbins (Fantagraphics, 2009)

Pretty in Ink: North American Women Cartoonists 1896–2013 by Trina Robbins (Fantagraphics, 2013)

LITTLE LULU
Plays
to Win
by Marge

Little Lulu was the official mascot of Kleenex until the early 1960s.
(Published in 1947. Courtesy Fantagraphics.)

MARJORIE HENDERSON BUELL

Golden Age • Cartoonist

Best known by her pen name **Marge, Marjorie Henderson Buell may be most recognized as the creator of the iconic comics character Little Lulu.** But with a keen business sense and firm understanding of American copyright law, she also stands as one of the first cartoonists to hold licensing and editorial control over her own work.

A true pioneer of her time, Buell made her cartooning debut in 1920 at the age of 16 with the publication of her drawings in *The Public Ledger* in Philadelphia and *For Boys and Girls*, where she garnered attention as a talented artist. In 1935, she received the offer of a lifetime from *The Saturday Evening Post* and signed on to submit single-panel wordless cartoons to the prestigious publication, replacing Carl Anderson's cartoon *Henry*.

What started as a single-panel cartoon depicting a precocious, curly-haired girl who "regularly beat out the boys" (Collins 1993) would later become the Little Lulu empire. For over a decade, Buell would contribute a weekly single-panel pantomime comic to the *Post*, recounting the silent pranks and fresh stunts of precious Little Lulu. Although the comic in the *Post* would end in 1944 (in part because the *Post* didn't like Buell's merchandising partnerships), Little Lulu's many adventures would be enjoyed by generations of readers in a syndicated comic strip that lasted until 1969 and a comic book series that was published until 1984. Buell did not create the comic strips or comic book, but she did maintain oversight of the brand. Buell's work is sometimes overlooked in favor of the well-regarded work of John Stanley, who worked on the Little Lulu comic from 1945 to 1959.

Throughout Little Lulu's many editorial incarnations, Buell made sure to retain the rights to her creation, which was unusual for the time. With the help of canny business partners, Buell would transform the pen and ink creation into a public brand. From showcasing Kleenex facial tissues as the company's mascot to numerous animated shorts on the big screen and merchandise, Little Lulu rose to fame as an American icon that is still loved and recognized to this day.

In light of her success with Little Lulu, Buell quickly became a star in the editorial cartooning circuit and would go on to produce work for other publications like *Collier's, Ladies' Home Journal,* and *Life.* Although her portfolio was diverse and extensive, Little Lulu would prove to be the cartoon that put Buell on the map both in terms of her art and her keen business sense.

Along with drawing the cartoons, Buell routinely reviewed and negotiated terms of use and accepted and declined deals with the guidance of her team. She was a business woman in the purest sense of the word during a time when women weren't seen as capable of navigating the ruthless and cutthroat world of capitalist America. Even when Buell made the decision to sell the character rights to Western Publishing for $99,000 in 1971, she made sure to include contractual language that would ensure that "Western recognizes the unique status of *Little Lulu* and associated and subordinated characters as copyright cartoons presenting a high level of entertainment and originality, disassociated from vulgar or crude ideas or unworthy products and agrees that future uses of the characters shall conform to said standards to the best of its ability" (Heintjes 2012).

Out of a love for her work and its integrity, Buell has inspired countless generations of women cartoonists and helped lay the foundation for what the comics industry embraces today as creator-owned works. In the early 1990s, Buell's popular creation inspired the name of Friends of Lulu, an organization that advocated for women in the comics industry. Co-founder Heidi MacDonald said the name was selected in part because it symbolized the ways in which "Lulu was always triumphing against the stupid things that boys did, but in an egalitarian way that didn't demean the boys as characters" (Robbins 2013). While both the comic and organization are no longer around (Friends of Lulu dissolved in 2011), Buell's legacy is still felt today as new generations of women become comics creators.

Pretty in Ink: North American Women Cartoonists 1896–2013 by Trina Robbins (Fantagraphics, 2013)

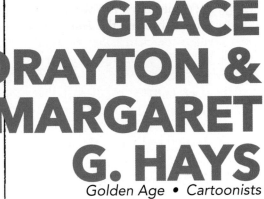

The Turr'ble Tales of Kaptin Kiddo

Told by the Boswell of childish romancers, Margaret G. Hays, and pictured by childhood's cleverest caricaturist, Grace G. Wiederseim.

If you don't laugh, you can't laugh when you see the pictures and read the first story in the SUNDAY OAKLAND TRIBUNE for August 29.

Copyright, 1909, by The North American Company.

THIS IS KAPTIN KIDDO

He's a "heap sight" funnier than he looks here, and, land knows, he looks funny enough!

GRACE DRAYTON & MARGARET G. HAYS

Golden Age • Cartoonists

An advertisement for *The Turr'ble Tales of Kaptin Kiddo*, co-created by Grace Drayton and Margaret G. Hays.
(Printed in *The Oakland Tribune*, August 26, 1909.)

Sister act Grace Drayton and Margaret Gebbie Hays' comics of cherubic, misbehaving children would help define not just the comics pages for decades, but would have a lasting impact in the world of advertising. Their influence can be felt even today, echoing in the Japanese style of kawaii, or cuteness.

Drayton, who worked for several years under her first husband's name Wiederseim, would begin her foray into the comics pages with *Naughty Toodles* (1903), becoming the first woman cartoonist on the Hearst Syndicate. Together, Drayton and Hays created *The Adventures of Dolly Drake and Bobby Blake in Storyland* (1905) and *The Turr'ble Tales of Kaptin Kiddo* (1909). Drayton and Hays' work featured cute, round-faced tots whose independent spirit meant they frequently found themselves in a tight spot. The dialogue reflected this cuteness, utilizing exaggerated baby talk and childish dialect.

Drayton would find her greatest fame in commercial art. In 1904, her then-husband Theodore Wiederseim submitted an advertising proposal to

Campbell's Soup that featured some of Drayton's wide-eyed children. Executives loved it, and Drayton's work was soon featured on streetcars and in prominent magazines like *Ladies' Home Journal* and *The Saturday Evening Post*.

Extremely childish at first, the Campbell kids eventually transitioned into more mature advocates for healthy eating and active lifestyles, and the characters remained a cornerstone of Campbell's advertising for decades. Shortly after launching the campaign, Campbell's soon recognized the merchandising potential of Drayton's work. She was enlisted to draw dozens of postcards, which inspired a line of dolls that is still sought after by collectors today.

Drayton and Hays' style of art was a hit at the turn of the 20th century and heavily influenced the comics pages and commercial art into the 1930s and 1940s. Drayton and Hays were contemporaries with Rose O'Neill, whose incredibly popular Kewpies were conceived around 1909, launched as toys in 1912, and helped fuel the market for cartoons and merchandise featuring angelic, apple-faced children.

Much of this merchandise found popularity outside of the United States, which likely influenced Japanese shōjo (girls') manga artists, including Matsumoto Katsuji, whose character Kurukuru Kurumi-chan (1938) reflected the style employed by Drayton, Hays, and O'Neill. When asked about the influences on the character, Matsumoto couldn't name a specific artist, but as Ryan Holmberg writes for *The Comics Journal*, Matsumoto's work bears the hallmarks of Drayton, Hays, and O'Neill's artistic style, with "exaggerated neotenic features and sartorial accouterments that are associated with Japanese kawaii: an oversized head, low wide-set eyes, fat truncated limbs, adorable hand gestures, bell dress, a ribbon in the hair" (2014).

Hays passed away in 1925, and Drayton passed away in 1936, one year after starting her final comics venture, *The Pussycat Princess*. Even after passing, their work was reproduced and emulated for decades, putting an indelible mark on the market for cuteness worldwide.

FURTHER READING

Pretty in Ink: North American Women Cartoonists 1896–2013 by Trina Robbins (Fantagraphics, 2013)

Edwina Dumm's *Tippie* follows the adventures of a mischievous boy and his shaggy dog.

(Dated 12/22, year of publication unknown. Edwina Dumm Collection, The Ohio State University Billy Ireland Cartoon Library & Museum.)

EDWINA DUMM

Golden Age • Cartoonist

Alongside fellow cartoonist suffragists like Nell Brinkley and Rose O'Neill, Edwina Dumm used her editorial work to fight for the rights of all women across the United States.

More than just a contributor to publications like *The Columbus Daily Monitor* and *Life* magazine, Dumm is also credited as being the first woman to work as a professional full-time editorial cartoonist and even possibly the first female political cartoonist in the United States.

Born in Ohio, Dumm got her start in 1915 by contributing cartoons as a staff artist for *The Columbus Daily Monitor*, where she drew spot illustrations, political portraits, and editorial cartoons. Inspired not only by the fantastic works of Lewis Carroll, but also by the timelier and socially relevant works of Mark Twain, Dumm developed a keen eye for observing the social and political world around her. Dumm had no problem tackling difficult subjects, ranging from prohibition and women's rights to the Mexican War and World War I. "I thought you had to know a lot about the politics of the past," recalls Dumm. "[But] all you had to know at that time—and possibly today—was what was going on that day and the policy of the paper" (Billy Ireland Cartoon Library & Museum).

The March 1916 issue of *Cartoons Magazine* heaped praise on Dumm (while misspelling her last name as "Dunn") and her work at the *Monitor*:

> It is not often that the ladies make a success of political cartooning, but Miss Edwina Dunn [sic], of the *Columbus Saturday Monitor*, refuses to be handicapped by precedent [sic]. No subject is too big for her to wrestle with, and in the pages of the *Monitor* she interprets world events in real masculine cartoons.

Like so many artists of the time, Dumm was drawn to New York City, where she moved in 1917 after the *Monitor* closed up shop. Dumm went to see George Matthew Adams, who led one of the largest cartoon syndicates at the time. Based on her work for the *Monitor*, Adams hired Dumm to create a daily cartoon six days a week (he didn't include the coveted Sunday spot).

Under the one-word moniker "Edwina," Dumm began the comic strip for which she would become most famous: *Cap Stubbs and Tippie*. The strip, which featured the misadventures of little boy Cap, his dog Tippie, and Cap's consternated parents and grandmother, began in 1918 and hit peak popularity during the Great Depression. It would eventually earn a spot on the Sunday pages in 1934. Given the popularity of Dumm's canine character over his human com-panions, the name of the strip was eventually shortened to just *Tippie*, and it ran until 1960. *Tippie* is considered to be the first continuity strip done by a woman (Robbins 2013).

A woman of immense talent and an impressive portfolio, Dumm wasn't limited to the funny pages. She illustrated numerous books, drew for *Tattler* and *Life* (including the cover for the January 1930 issue of the latter), and later in her life did "subway sketches," painted while she rode the subways of New York. "Edwina paved the way as the first woman employed in a full time position as editorial cartoonist," the Billy Ireland Cartoon Library & Museum notes. "Her art was funny, heartwarming, inspirational, and a landmark in cartooning history."

In 1950, Dumm was among the first three women to be admitted to the National Cartoonists Society, along with Barbara Shermund and Hilda Terry. In 1978, Dumm earned another distinction that no other woman had received before: the Gold Key Award from the National Cartoonists Society Hall of Fame.

Dumm retired from cartooning in 1966. In 1990, at the age of 96, Dumm passed away in New York, but her work continues to stand as a reminder of the immense impact she had on the cartooning world. From humor to human rights, Dumm set the stage and inspired generations of future cartoonists, male and female alike.

FURTHER READING

Pretty in Ink: North American Women Cartoonists 1896–2013 by Trina Robbins (Fantagraphics, 2013)

A SPORTING DECISION

Ethel Hays' artwork for the January 13, 1935, edition of *Everyweek*.

(International Museum of Cartoon Art Collection, The Ohio State University Billy Ireland Cartoon Library & Museum.)

ETHEL HAYS
Golden Age • Syndicated Cartoonist

"A real feather in the feminist's cap." This is how one newspaper described cartoonist Ethel Hays in a 1928 article (Robbins 2013)—a description that to this day remains an apt portrayal of the can-do woman who would not only become one of the most prolific commercial artists of the early 1900s, but whose work would epitomize and capture the nuances of a new generation of young, strong, and classy women coming into their independence in the 1920s.

Born in 1892 in Billings, Montana, no one ever doubted Hays' incredible talent. The illustrations that she drew for her high school newspaper, the art classes she led for wounded WWI veterans, and the numerous art school scholarships she was awarded saw Hays being recognized by major institutions and newspaper publishers from Los Angeles to New York City.

From 1923 to the 1950s, Hays would contribute to some of the most popular strips, producing some of the most iconic cartoons in print. *Vic and Ethel* (later called *Ethel*), *Flapper Fanny*, *Femininities*, and *Maryanne* were just a few of the cartoons on which Hays worked, and many appeared in daily newspapers alongside each other. Within her first year with the Newspaper Enterprise Association syndicate, it is estimated that Hays' work appeared in over 500 newspapers—a staggering presence for any cartoonist of the time, regardless of gender.

Her saucy wit, playful sense of humor, and knack for commenting on the lives of young American women made Hays an outstanding writer. But it was her clean, energetic, Art Deco-inspired artwork that really captured the eyes of readers. While young ladies casually perusing Hays' *Flapper Fanny* cartoon basked in what it meant to be a newly independent woman of the world, young men scrabbled through the cartoons to find out the secrets of the independent women they were trying to court. "Hays'

combination of superb artwork and comedic sensibilities added up to a formula that few female cartoonists of the time could claim," writes Tom Heintjes (2012). "She created a feature popular with both men and women."

In the late 1940s and 1950s, when the comics industry came under attack by *Seduction of the Innocent* author Dr. Fredric Wertham and the anti-comics crusade was in full force, Hays saw an opportunity to retire from her editorial work, but she didn't leave cartooning entirely. Ever driven, Hays would go on to illustrate educational children's books (most notably several *Raggedy Ann and Andy* books), coloring books, and even paper doll cut-out books until her death at the age of 97 in 1989.

In a time when women cartoonists were often given only two genres to work within—cute animal stories or romance cartoons—Hays showed the cartooning world that even within these boundaries women could be exceptional and overcome gender biases. As Heintjes notes:

> Ethel Hays worked in the era's standard female genres yet rose above them. Her talent for cartooning was so great that her work had universal appeal even while working well within the accepted limitations.

Although she was influenced by other women cartoonists, like Nell Brinkley, Hays' fluid art style and independent voice in turn influenced other cartoonists, both women and men.

FURTHER READING

Pretty in Ink: North American Women Cartoonists 1896–2013 by Trina Robbins (Fantagraphics, 2013)

"Your father," she said grimly, "has bought an automobile."

One of Hokinson's illustrations for *How Dear to My Heart* by Emily Kimbrough.
(Dodd, Mead & Company, 1944.)

HELEN HOKINSON

Golden Age • Cartoonists

From the earliest days of *The New Yorker* in 1925, founding editor Harold Ross was well aware that his stable of talented cartoonists, essayists, and humorists made him "the luckiest son of a bitch alive" (Harvey 2013).

Ross cited four contributors for his publication's success: E.B. White, James Thurber, Peter Arno, and cartoonist Helen Hokinson, a "first-class character artist."

Hokinson was born in 1893 in the small town of Mendota, Illinois. By high school, she had already established her lifelong habit of toting a sketchbook everywhere she went, producing humorous sketches of classmates and teachers. Around 1913, she enrolled in a two-year program in fashion illustration and design at the Chicago Academy of Fine Arts. After graduation she found some work with department stores and art agencies in Chicago, but soon moved to New York City with plans to launch a career in fashion illustration.

Unsurprisingly, Hokinson did not abandon her trusty sketchbook in New York. She even once brought the sketchbook into a Turkish bath, to the alarm of the nude clientele. When she took a course from Howard Giles at the School of Fine and Applied Arts (now the Parsons School of Design), he recognized her talent for capturing personality and humor in sketches from life and encouraged her to submit some work to magazines. Hokinson chose the newly-hatched *New Yorker*, which first published Hokinson on July 4, 1925, and would continue to feature at least one of her cartoons nearly every week for the next 25 years, a grand total of over 1,700 cartoons.

Initially Hokinson's cartoons were printed just as she submitted them, without captions, but *The New Yorker* editors soon began assigning writers to add punchlines. Before long, she struck up an exclusive collaboration with James Reid Parker, a fellow contributor to the magazine who appreciated her visual perspicacity and who had a knack for capturing her sense of humor in a short phrase.

Hokinson quickly found a favorite subject for her work: the plump upper-class society matron "with nothing much to do except shop, try new odd ventures such as fencing, look for maids, and go to club meetings," wrote later *New Yorker* cartoonist Liza Donnelly (2005). Although her "girls" were invariably the butt of the joke in each piece, Hokinson was fiercely fond of them and insisted that they were not stupid but simply misguided and perhaps a bit flighty.

She was so disturbed by public misconception of the girls, in fact, that in the late 1940s she overcame her natural shyness enough to embark on a speaking tour in their defense. Tragically, while landing at Washington National Airport on November 1, 1949, the passenger jet in which she was riding collided in midair with another plane. All lost their lives. The next issue of *The New Yorker* carried a mournful editors' note:

[T]he ladies she drew have become perhaps the most widely known and certainly the most affectionately cherished of any characters we have introduced to our readers. If satire is defined as an exposure of anyone's weakness, she was not a satirist at all, or even a humorist, if there is any implication of harshness in that. Her work was the product of loving observation and a boundless delight in all absurdity, none more than that she found in herself, and the pleasure she gave other people was really a reflection of her own. We can remember no unhappier duty than writing this final paragraph about an irreplaceable artist and a woman whom some of us have fondly admired half our lives. (Harvey 2013)

Pretty in Ink: North American Women Cartoonists 1896–2013 by Trina Robbins (Fantagraphics, 2013)

Brenda Starr, Reporter was a reflection of Dale Messick herself.
(Published July 7, 1940. Courtesy Fantagraphics.)

DALE MESSICK
Golden Age • Syndicated Cartoonist

Throughout her life Dale Messick, one of the first nationally-syndicated American woman cartoonists, expanded possibilities both for real women in her own profession and for fictional women in the comics pages. Messick's jet-setting reporter Brenda Starr was an ambitious career woman when most of her female comics page neighbors were housewives, and the creator herself blazed a trail for other women who came after her in the industry.

Dalia Messick was born in 1906 in South Bend, Indiana, the oldest of five children. Encouraged to develop her creative skills by her father, a sign painter and art teacher, and her mother, a milliner, she drew her first comic at 10 years old. After high school, she briefly attended the Ray Commercial Art School in Chicago during the Great Depression, but soon took a job drawing greeting cards to support her parents and younger brothers. Within a short time she shrewdly increased her salary from $10 a week to $35 by negotiating progressively higher rates at different companies, but she quit in 1934 after "one of her cards sold a bumper-crop of copies and she didn't receive a bonus," according to a profile in *Animation World Magazine* (Leger 2000).

Messick then moved to New York City and found work at yet another greeting card company, still sending half of her $50-per-week salary back home. In the evenings she developed concepts and art for newspaper comic strips, which she then offered to various papers and syndicates without success. Suspecting that editors didn't take her work seriously because of her sex, she began working under the name Dale during this period. In 1940 she finally sold *Brenda Starr, Reporter* to the Chicago Tribune–New York News Syndicate, making her the first American woman creator of a nationally-syndicated comic strip.

Like her creator, the character Brenda Starr was ahead of her time. At the time, women in journalism were mostly relegated to the society pages and advice columns. The same had been true for Brenda, Messick said, but she was determined to break out of that mold: "she was already a reporter when the strip started, but she was sick and tired of covering nothing but ice-cream socials. She wanted a job with action, like the men reporters had" (Severo 2005).

Brenda got that excitement and then some: at various times she parachuted out of a plane with no pilot, was hijacked by pirates on the high seas, and went undercover to join a girl gang, all while coiffed and dressed to the height of fashion. In fact, during Messick's 40-year tenure on *Brenda Starr*, women journalists often complained of its complete inauthenticity, to which she cheerfully replied that no one would read the strip if it depicted the actual life of a reporter.

Messick and Brenda also sometimes pushed the boundaries of what was allowed in newspaper comics at the time. Brenda's voluptuous figure and red hair were inspired by Rita Hayworth, but *The Washington Post* obituary of Messick recalled that whenever she "drew in cleavage or a navel, the syndicate would erase it. She was once banned in Boston after showing Brenda smoking a polka-dot cigar" (Sullivan 2005). Even in post-Brenda semi-retirement, Messick's strip *Granny Glamour* was reportedly rejected by AARP's *Modern Maturity* magazine because the senior citizen characters were "too activist" (Sullivan 2005). That weekly strip instead found a home in *Oakmont Gardens*, a magazine for the California retirement community where Messick was living by that time.

Messick drew *Brenda Starr* until 1980, when the syndicate pressured her to retire from art duties, and she continued writing the storyline until 1983. The strip lived on until 2010 under two successive writer-artist teams, all women. In 1998, at 92 years old, Messick received the National Cartoonists Society's Milton Caniff Lifetime Achievement Award, which she called "the greatest moment of my life" (Luther 2005). She died at age 98 in 2005 in California.

FURTHER READING

Brenda Starr, Reporter: The Collected Daily and Sunday Newspaper Strips Volume 1 by Dale Messick (Hermes Press, 2012)

Pretty in Ink: North American Women Cartoonists 1896–2013 by Trina Robbins (Fantagraphics, 2013)

This single panel from Tarpé Mills' *Miss Fury* led to the cancellation of the strip from newspapers around the country. Subsequent reprints often censored it.

(Published March 21, 1943. Courtesy The Library of American Comics / IDW Publishing.)

TARPÉ MILLS

Golden Age • Cartoonist

With a knack for contemporary fashion and keen sense of strong character development, June Mills adopted the pseudonym Tarpé Mills to conceal her gender. She is credited as the creator of the first major costumed female protagonist in the contemporary comics industry—Miss Fury, which predated DC Comics' Wonder Woman by a few months.

In April 1941, Mills' iconic character debuted in her own dedicated newspaper comic strip published by Bell Syndicate. Originally called *Black Fury*, Mills' effortlessly stylish socialite by day and black catsuit–clad crime fighter by night, Marla Drake (a.k.a. Miss Fury) was a fantastically empowered female character the likes of which the comics industry had never seen before. Mills quickly garnered popular acclaim from both male and female comics fans.

In a time when most women characters were one-dimensional pieces of arm candy for muscle-bound male superheroes, Mills introduced an array of female characters imbued with their own unique complexities and strong senses of feminine strength. From the justice seeker Miss Fury to the numerous *femmes fatales* she fought, Mills created not only the first, and to this day one of the industry's most beloved costumed superheroines, but also some of the most salacious (and sought after) women villains of the Golden Age. Although Mills initially used her pen name to gain access into the industry, she recalled in a 1940s interview that "it would have been a major letdown to the kids if they found out that the author of such virile and awesome characters was a gal" (Robbins 1993).

Despite her accolades and popularity, Mills was often criticized for the revealing costumes in *Miss Fury*. In fact, a panel in her March 21, 1943, strip that showed Miss Fury in the equivalent of a bikini immediately led to the cancellation of the strip in 37 newspapers (Robbins 1993). Despite the controversy, there was no denying that both *Miss Fury* and Tarpé Mills had secured a special space in pop culture and the comics industry. Voted a fan favorite and "unanimously acclaimed" by *The Chicago Sun*, *Miss Fury* strips would be remain syndicated in numerous newspapers across the United States and reprinted in comic book form by Timely. Miss Fury's popularity as a wartime heroine would also extend to featured articles in *Time* and *The Miami Daily Herald*—something simply unheard of during the time.

When the *Miss Fury* strip ended in 1952, Mills mostly retired from comics, but she didn't stop entirely. In 1971, she took up work with Marvel to illustrate the seven-page romance comic *Our Love Story*. She would also work on an independent graphic novel project *Albino Jo, the Man with the Tiger Eyes*, which recounted the adventures of one of Miss Fury's crime-fighting friends. Sadly, the latter work was incomplete when Mills died in 1988.

Miss Fury remains Tarpé Mills' most notable work—a character that has been drawn and redrawn numerous times from the 1940s to today by both men and women. Mills never sacrificed a strong, multidimensional female protagonist in favor of sexy, one-sided vixens. And though the times initially forced her to adopt a pseudonym to hide her gender from biased publishers and readers, in the end Mills was able to stand strong as one of the female creators that paved the way for future women to work in comics and the superhero genre.

FURTHER READING

Tarpé Mills & Miss Fury Sensational Sundays 1944–1949 edited by Trina Robbins (IDW, 2011)

Tarpé Mills & Miss Fury Sensational Sundays 1941–1944 edited by Trina Robbins (IDW, 2011)

Pretty in Ink: North American Women Cartoonists 1896–2013 by Trina Robbins (Fantagraphics, 2013)

CUPID ON EASTER.

THE Lenten days were trials sore,
  Me from my Love absenting;
I dared not knock upon the door
  Where Phyllis was repenting—
Where she who ne'er knew aught of sin
Did sweet, vain penances within.

In sackcloth bowed the Lovely Maid,
  Renouncing Earth's urbanities;
Forswearing Joy with drooping head
  And Love and all the Vanities;
While she, the Kind and Gracious One,
Dropped tears for kindnesses undone.

But now some comfort doth she take
  When Easter morn is glowing,
Fresh toilette and resolves doth make,
  Then off to Church is going,
Where her sister-angels guide her
And — I kneel once more beside her.
                    O'Neill Latham.

"Cupid on Easter,"
features the cherubic figures that characterized
O'Neill's illustrations.

(Published in *Puck Magazine* on April 4,
1901. From the Bonniebrook Museum
collection.)

ROSE O'NEILL
Golden Age • Illustrator

Despite limitations imposed upon women at
the turn of the century, faith in her craft and the firm belief
that women weren't meant to be silenced made Rose O'Neill
arguably the first American woman cartoonist to be professionally published. During a time when editorial illustration was strictly
a man's business, the self-taught artist, women's rights activist, and creator
of the internationally recognizable cartoon cherub Kewpie would rise to

fame and become one of the best known and highest paid female commercial artists at the turn of the 20th century.

Born in Wilkes-Barre, Pennsylvania, in 1874, O'Neill had a fondness for illustration from an early age. At age 19, O'Neill set out to seek professional work in New York City. Equipped with only 60 illustrations in her portfolio, O'Neill's work quickly gained the attention of esteemed male magazine editors and advertising executives despite her gender.

By 1896, O'Neill had produced over 700 cartoons and illustrations for the popular satire magazine *Puck*, and through-

out her 20s, she amassed an incredibly large and diverse portfolio of commercial work and an equally impressive client list—a set of accomplishments few could claim, man or woman, in the world of illustration. A woman ahead of her time, "O'Neill's appeal was due to a combination of her sense of humor and her romantic nature," notes the Bonniebrook Museum, O'Neill's former home and a repository for much of her work. "It didn't hurt that she could work quickly and meet deadlines."

Harper's, Life, Cosmopolitan, Collier's, Ladies' Home Journal, Good Housekeeping, and *Women's Home Companion* were just a few of publications to which O'Neill contributed, and her work for Kellogg's Cornflakes, Jell-O, Edison Phonograph, and Rock Island Railroad could be seen in advertisements across the nation. It was the approximately 100 illustrations that she did for Jell-O from 1909 to 1922 and her own infamous cartoon creation Kewpie, though, that would make O'Neill a household name and a conduit for women's rights.

O'Neill used her artistic talents to campaign for the equality of women and minorities across the U.S. Through her celebrity and art, O'Neill was able to speak for underrepresented populations. Her art amplified women's rights in a way never before seen by the American public. Her drive and how she used her art to fight for political equality remains part of Rose O'Neill's legacy to this day.

O'Neill's eternally popular Kewpies adorned posters and postcards in support of the women's suffrage movement.
(Printed in 1915 by Campbell Art Company for the National Woman Suffrage Pub. Co. Inc. Courtesy Catherine H. Palczewski Postcard Archive, University of Northern Iowa, Cedar Falls, IA.)

FURTHER READING

Pretty in Ink: North American Women Cartoonists 1896–2013 by Trina Robbins (Fantagraphics, 2013)

Jackie Ormes at work on
Torchy in Heartbeats.
(Courtesy Nancy Goldstein.)

JACKIE ORMES
Golden Age • Syndicated Cartoonist

Zelda Jackson Ormes, better known as **Jackie, was the first Black woman to make a living as a cartoonist.** Between 1937 and 1955, her strips were syndicated extensively nationwide in the Black press, featuring Black women in roles and social situations they were never accorded in the mainstream media of the day.

Ormes got her start in journalism while she was still in high school, reporting for the *Pittsburgh Courier*, which had nationwide distribution. In 1937 Ormes tried her hand at cartooning with her first strip, *Torchy Brown in Dixie to Harlem.* Through Torchy, a Southern transplant to New York who became a performer at the Cotton Club, Ormes was able to address not only racism and prejudice, but also women's careers and other issues she felt strongly about. She later described herself as "anti-war [and] anti-everything that's smelly" (Jackson 1985). *Torchy Brown* initially appeared only in the *Pittsburgh Courier*, but was soon syndicated in 14 more Black papers across the country.

In 1940 Ormes brought the original *Torchy Brown* to an end and briefly moved with her husband Earl to his small hometown of Salem, Ohio, but she

art to match a male writer's storylines. This did not work out well, as Ormes said she constantly had to remind the writer that her character "was no moon-struck crybaby, and that she wouldn't perish between heartbreaks. I have never liked dreamy little women who can't hold their own" (Jackson 1985). Eventually Ormes regained full creative control over the strip, which ran until 1955, when Black papers cut their comics sections to cover the growing Civil Rights Movement. Ormes switched to fine art painting until she had to give that up due to rheumatoid arthritis.

By the time Ormes retired from comics, her husband was managing the historic DuSable Hotel on Chicago's South Side, hosting a veritable who's who of Black performers, artists, and writers. Ormes also was heavily involved in advocacy through the Chicago Urban League and the South Side Community Art Center.

Ormes died in 1985. While her work engaged and inspired confidence in Black women, her own industry remains virtually off limits to them. From 1989 to 2005, there was exactly one nationally-syndicated Black woman newspaper cartoonist, *Where I'm Coming From* creator Barbara Brandon-Croft, who credits Ormes as an inspiration. Any potential successors have apparently been stifled not only by the familiar combination of racism and sexism, but also by syndicates' heavy reliance on rerunning strips by deceased or retired creators.

was unhappy there. They soon moved to Chicago. There, Ormes got a reporting job with the *Chicago Defender*. In 1946 she started another single-panel strip, *Patty-Jo 'n' Ginger*, which featured the acerbic little girl Patty-Jo and her fashion-plate older sister Ginger. Through the voice of Patty-Jo, Ormes again commented on issues of the day, such as racism, sexism, the military-industrial complex, and McCarthyism. In 1948 she licensed a Patty-Jo doll, which was the first nationally distributed Black doll and remains a collector's item today.

In 1950 a national syndicate persuaded Ormes to bring back Torchy Brown for a new strip, *Torchy in Heartbeats*. Initially, the syndicate only wanted her to provide

FURTHER READING

Jackie Ormes: The First African American Woman Cartoonist by Nancy Goldstein (University of Michigan Press, 2008)

Lou Rogers often criticized the criminalization of birth control.

(From Margaret Sanger's *Birth Control Review*, July 1918.)

LOU ROGERS
Golden Age • Political Cartoonist

When Lou Rogers first tried to break into political cartooning around 1908, "Editors said there were no women cartoonists," a reporter and childhood friend recalled about 15 years later. "They said women couldn't even draw jokes. They hadn't any humor" (*Lewiston Daily Sun* 1924). The naysayers were almost right on one score: Rogers was indeed among the first female professional cartoonists in the United States. But on the other points, she soon proved them wrong, building a decades-long career through hard work and sheer determination.

Annie Lucasta Rogers was one of seven siblings raised on a farm in northern Maine. Rogers showed an early talent for caricature, becoming "the bane of teachers and the delight of her classmates," she recalled later in an autobiographical essay for *The Nation* (1989). She taught school in rural Maine just long enough to save up money to enroll at the Massachusetts Normal Art

School (now the Massachusetts College of Art and Design) in Boston. An admittedly undisciplined student, Rogers' college fund lasted for a year and a half.

While in Boston, Rogers developed a keen interest in physical culture, a movement that promoted exercise among the masses. She left art school and embarked on what she later called a "tramp adventure," teaching fitness classes in Chicago and points west. Shortly thereafter she returned east with a single ambition: becoming a cartoonist.

Rogers never liked her given name and already went by Lou, which turned out to be "a tremendous help in the days when editors were so prejudiced they could not see humor in a cartoon if they first saw a feminine name attached." Before long, Rogers was selling "joke stuff to all sorts of magazines and newspapers and syndicates" (*Lewiston Daily Sun* 1924).

Rogers' pet issue, unsurprisingly for an independent woman in the 1910s, was women's suffrage. Around this time she undertook another extraordinary journey, traveling around New York and New Jersey for several months, giving what she called "cartoon speeches" for the National Woman Suffrage Association (NWSA). Armed with a folding platform-and-easel contraption built by her brother, she expounded on votes for women while also drawing cartoons. Rogers was accustomed to being heckled or even pelted with eggs during her cartoon speeches, but even her detrac-

tors were soon captivated by the show since "all people are like little children when it comes to watching a picture grow on a piece of white paper," she observed (Sheppard 1985).

Back in New York City, Rogers landed regular gigs in NWSA's *Woman's Journal* and the *New York Call*. In 1912, when *Judge* started a "Modern Woman" page about suffrage issues, Rogers was the main cartoonist. The publication's art editor Grant Hamilton enthused that "she has what ninety-nine out of a hundred lack, the ability to see the way to get the idea into the picture" (Sheppard 1985).

Rogers' devotion to feminist causes did not wane after the 19th Amendment finally passed. In 1918 she joined Margaret Sanger's *Birth Control Review* as one of three art editors. After leaving that position in 1922, she created a full-color children's feature called "The Gimmicks" for *Ladies' Home Journal*, and continued to work on illustrations for decades. She died in 1952 at age 72.

"Tearing Off the Bonds,"
from *Judge Magazine*.
(Printed October 19, 1912.)

TEARING OFF THE BONDS.

FURTHER READING

Birth Control Review online archive
http://birthcontrolreview.net/

One of Shermund's illustrations for the Armed Services Edition of *My Family Right or Wrong*, by John Philip Sousa III.
(Printed in 1943. Courtesy of The Bancroft Library, University of California, Berkeley.)

BARBARA SHERMUND

Golden Age • Cartoonist

Within the first four months of its existence, *The New Yorker* took on a number of talented cartoonists, including women. Among them was San Francisco-born Barbara Shermund, who was one of the first women admitted to the National Cartoonists Society but whose work remains regrettably underappreciated today.

Shermund attended the California School of Fine Arts, encouraged by her architect father and sculptor mother to pursue her artistic talent. She moved to New York City at age 26, soon finding a place at *The New Yorker*, where she would contribute nearly 600 drawings between 1926 and 1944, when her last *New Yorker* cartoon ran. She worked in a variety of styles and mediums, including block prints, washes, inks, and lithographs, sometimes employing very bold lines and at other times using a sketchier style.

While Shermund wasn't the only woman at *The New Yorker*, she was one of the most outspoken feminists and originally relied almost entirely on her own ideas. In her history of the women of *The New Yorker*, Liza Donnelly describes Shermund's work:

> She drew mostly about the New Woman, demonstrating an understanding of the newfound independence while not being afraid to poke fun at her. Her women were alternately clueless and strong, depending on the cartoon. This was the state of women at that time—some were experimenting, coming out of the home, speaking their mind. Meanwhile, the flappers among them showed disdain for an education and just wanted to have fun.

It was clear that "Shermund's women did not need men" (Donnelly 2005), and they were often more independent and resilient than the women characters portrayed in cartoons by her contemporaries. Shermund was both well-traveled and forward-thinking, which appealed to editors at *The New Yorker*, who were keen on exploring gender politics. Many of Shermund's cartoons reflected this attitude. Further, Shermund had no qualms about targeting both men and women in her cartoons, commenting on topics ranging from male sexism and infidelity to the ways in which women tried to attract men.

Over time, Shermund's style and voice changed, due in no small part to the fact that she began to employ gag writers to write ideas and captions for her. As Donnelly writes, "Thus her work changed from the breezy feminist attitude evident in her captions to stereotypes that fit prevailing trends." The 1930s were also marked by fewer opportunities for women creators and an increasing trend toward depicting women in unflattering ways. During this period, Shermund began contributing cartoons to *Esquire*, which was less discerning than *The New Yorker*. Shermund's *Esquire* cartoons tended toward the coarse humor preferred by the publication's audience, and Shermund fell into the prevailing pattern of mocking women.

Around this time, editors at *The New Yorker* tried to address what they perceived as a reduction in quality in Shermund's cartoons. Shermund had begun to rely more and more on gag writers, and the relationship soured further until Shermund parted ways with the publication in 1944. She continued to work for *Esquire* and King Features Syndicate for a few more decades, but she passed away in obscurity in 1978.

Shermund's work is overlooked today, undoubtedly in part because her later reliance on gag writers overshadowed her more impactful early work, and she is deserving of more recognition. Regardless, Shermund did have another notable accomplishment: she joined Edwina Dumm and Hilda Terry in the inaugural class of women who joined the National Cartoonists Society in 1950.

FURTHER READING

Funny Ladies: The New Yorker's Greatest Women Cartoonists And Their Cartoons by Liza Donnelly (Prometheus Books, 2005)

The second appearance of Aqualad, one of Ramona Fradon's many contributions to Aquaman.

(From "Aquaman: The Menace of Aqualad," *Adventure Comics* #270, March 1960. Courtesy DC Comics.)

RAMONA FRADON

Silver Age • Cartoonist

For a long stretch during the Silver Age of comics, Ramona Fradon was one of only two women artists working on superheroes.

Over a long career drawing Aquaman, Metamorpho, Plastic Man, and the drastically different newspaper comic *Brenda Starr, Reporter*, among many others, she has earned praise and recognition from others in the industry, such as Jon Morris, who said that her character designs for Metamorpho "convey [the relationships between characters] in a manner so perfectly executed and nuanced that I honestly believe they're the best-realized character designs in the entire genre of superhero comics" (Reed 2014).

Fradon was born in 1926. She studied at the New York Art Students' League and Parsons School of Design, graduating from the latter in 1950. Newly married and "very poor," she was encouraged to try her hand at comics. In a 2000 interview with Katherine Keller, she recalled: "I went out and bought a whole bunch of comic books and spent a couple of weeks reading them. I did a page of Western action shots and took them up to DC and got a job."

Her first work at DC was penciling and inking the Shining Knight story "Gadget Boom in Camelot" in *Adventure Comics* #165. A few issues later, Shining Knight was replaced by Aquaman, and Fradon became one of the principal artists for that character for the next 10 years. In 1960 she and writer Robert Bernstein co-created the Atlantean king's sidekick Aqualad. At the time, Fradon and Marie Severin at Marvel were the only women artists working on superhero comics.

Fradon most enjoyed drawing characters with a humorous edge, as opposed to the more serious superheroes, which she saw as "cardboard figures punching each other" (Keller 2000). After a few years away from comics to raise her daughter, she briefly returned to DC in 1965 to co-create Metamorpho with writer Bob Haney. Fradon then returned to childrearing full time until the mid-1970s, when she returned to DC and worked on another quirky character, Plastic Man. She also penciled most issues of *Super Friends* (1976–1981).

In 1980 Fradon made the leap to news-paper comics, taking over the illustration of *Brenda Starr, Reporter* from its original creator Dale Messick. The Tribune Media Services Syndicate made a stipulation that was unconventional to say the least: half of Messick's annual pension was deducted from Fradon's salary. Because Messick's separation from the strip was less than voluntary, Fradon said the older woman was "so angry at the syndicate that she vowed to live forever so that she could keep collecting that pension" (Keller 2000). Messick was still going strong 15 years later, when Fradon left the strip, and she ultimately lived to 98 years of age.

Although Fradon found important differences between comic books and newspaper comics, noting that it could be "somewhat discouraging to see all of the work you have done reduced to the size of a postage stamp" (Dueben 2013), she enjoyed depicting the life of a working mother like herself and especially loved hearing from women who had been fans of Brenda Starr over the years, including, she recalled, "one or two prominent women journalists [who] said that they were inspired by Brenda's example to become reporters."

Now entering her ninth decade, Fradon is still taking commissions and is a frequent guest on the convention circuit, where she continues to "love meeting fans" (Keller 2000).

FURTHER READING

The Art of Ramona Fradon by Ramona Fradon and Howard Chaykin (Dynamite, 2014)

Pretty in Ink: North American Women Cartoonists 1896–2013 by Trina Robbins (Fantagraphics, 2013)

Marie Severin's work was imbued with humor, which can be seen in the writing, pencils, and inks she did throughout Marvel's *Not Brand Echh.*

("How to Be a Comic Artist" from *Not Brand Echh* #11, December 1968. Courtesy Marvel Comics.)

MARIE SEVERIN
Silver Age • Cartoonist & Colorist

"First Lady of Comics" Marie Severin, an award-winning artist and colorist, has led one of the most interesting lives in the American comic book industry. Despite the myth that the industry was no place for a gal, her numerous achievements both in pre-Comics Code comics as well as Silver Age mainstream superhero fare proved time and time again that comics were in no way simply a boys' club.

In the 1950s, Severin fought alongside the EC group when the crusade against comics was in full force. In the 1960s, she would replace Steve Ditko and Bill Everett as the artist on Marvel's *Doctor Strange* and would co-create Spider-Woman, costume and all. In the 1970s until her retirement, Severin conquered almost every genre of comic book she tackled, from horror to humor. To editor Al Feldstein she was "the conscience of EC" (Jacobs 1972), to Stan Lee she was "Mirthful Marie" (Cassell 2012), and she remains one of the most acclaimed woman cartoonists in comics history.

Severin grew up in New York, the birthplace of the comics industry and lived with a family of artists. Her father was a trained artist from the Pratt Institute, her mother dabbled in illustration, and her brother John Severin was an EC artist. "I just took it for granted that's what one did in this house, so I did," noted the artist in an interview (Robbins 2013).

When Severin took on work at the EC offices in the late 1940s, the homegrown artist fit right in, never missing a beat in the frantic atmosphere of a publication house that prided itself not only of producing the best comics, but embracing free expression. Although EC is often remembered for creating some of the most striking and gruesome horror scenes ever printed in four colors, the same freedom given to artists was extended to then-colorist Severin, who is credited with using her personal color craft to bring a more tasteful atmosphere to the guts and gore.

"What I would do very often is, if somebody was being dismembered, I would rather color it in yellow because it's garish, and also you could see what was going on," recalls Severin in an interview with Dewey Cassell, adding:

"Or red, for the blood element, but not to subdue the artwork. If it was too complicated with these gory scenes, I'd rather put one color on it because, number one, you can see more… Frankly, I'd rather color with solids for, like, a murder scene, and yellow so you can see

everything. I wasn't trying to hide it. I mean, the main reason these people were buying these books was to see somebody's head cut off, y'know? Lose fingers and everything." (2012)

When the 1954 Senate Subcommittee Hearings all but forced the closure of EC and decimated the comics industry, Severin didn't close shop. She went to Marvel. She became a staff artist, working on Doctor Strange, Captain America, Sub-Mariner, Incredible Hulk, Marvel's satire magazine *Not Brand Echh*, and more. At Marvel, Severin was an inker, penciller, colorist, and art director.

"Marie Severin, wide brown eyes hidden behind her glasses, dressed in what Robin Green described as "very Peck & Peck," held her own against both the boys' club and the fans, all of whom she targeted in brilliant, wicked caricatures that were pinned up all around the [Marvel] office," writes journalist Sean Howe.

Severin's talent, positive attitude, and striking sense of humor saw her moving around the Marvel office just like any other creator. She wasn't the demure, fragile female secretary that took notes and managed the important people's schedules; she was one of the important people in the bullpen. Severin was a woman of the mainstream comics scene, and she dominated. Severin truly is the First Lady of comics.

FURTHER READING

Marie Severin: The Mirthful Mistress of Comics by Dewey Cassell with Aaron Sultan (TwoMorrows, 2012)

Marvel Masterworks: Not Brand Echh Volume 1 by various (Marvel, 2015)

Hilda Terry's *Teena* was the first cartoon to cater to the interests of teenage girls.

(Cover artwork for A-1 #15, featuring *Teena*. Published August 1948.)

HILDA TERRY
Silver Age • Syndicated Cartoonist

Imagine your first comic strip came about at the direct request of newspaper magnate William Randolph Hearst. This was Hilda Terry's reality in the early 1940s. Terry would eventually be among the first women to join the exclusive boys' club that was the National Cartoonists Society (holding the door open for other women behind her), and help pioneer the field of scoreboard animation.

Hilda Terry began her career as a cartoonist for *The Saturday Evening Post* and other magazines. Her work caught the eye of William Randolph Hearst, who telegraphed subordinates, demanding that they "Get Hilda Terry" for his comics pages (Miller 2006). In 1941, Terry's first feature, *It's a Girl's Life*, ran for King Features. One of the very few comics (and for a long time, the only comic) to focus specifically on the interests of teen girls, the strip would eventually be retitled *Teena* and run in newspapers until 1964.

Terry's husband, Gregory D'Alessio, nominated her to the National Cartoonists Society. At the time, the organization was exclusively male, and members hesitated to include women, presumably because "men wouldn't be able to curse" (Robbins 2013). Terry didn't hesitate to demand that the organization either rename itself or admit women. Her scathingly funny letter to NCS read:

Gentlemen:

While we are, individually, in complete sympathy with your wish to convene unhampered by the presence of women, and while we would, individually, like to continue, as far as we are concerned, the indulgence of your masculine whim, we find that the cost of your stag privilege is stagnation for us, professionally. Therefore, we appeal to you, in all fairness, to consider that:

WHEREAS there is no information in the title to denote that it is exclusively a men's organisation, and

WHEREAS a professional organisation that excludes women in this day and age is unheard of and unthought of, and

WHEREAS the public is therefore left to assume, where they are interested in any cartoonist of the female sex, that said cartoonist must be excluded from your exhibitions for other reasons damaging to the cartoonists professional prestige,

We most humbly request that you either alter your title to the National Men Cartoonists Society, or confine your activities to social and private functions, or discontinue, in effect, whatever rule or practice you have which bars otherwise qualified women cartoonists to membership for purely sexual reasons.

Sincerely,
The Committee for Women Cartoonists
Hilda Terry, temporary chairwoman

Even though Terry met some resistance from a handful of NCS members, she had the support of majority, including Milton Caniff (*Terry and the Pirates*) and Al Capp (*Li'l Abner*), so the boys' club came to an end. Terry was admitted to NCS alongside Edwina Dumm and Barbara Shermund, and she shortly began nominating her fellow women cartoonists for admission.

After a few years of freelance illustration, Terry left comics for baseball—that is, the burgeoning field of scoreboard animation. The very same organization that she once had to convince to admit her, the National Cartoonists Society, awarded her its Best Animation Cartoonist award in 1979 for her giant animated portraits of baseball players.

Terry effectively retired from animation and illustration in the 1980s, but she continued to teach at the Art Students League, where she herself learned art and met her husband, and she maintained an active online presence until her death in 2006 at the age of 92.

FURTHER READING

Pretty in Ink: North American Women Cartoonists 1896–2013 by Trina Robbins (Fantagraphics, 2013)

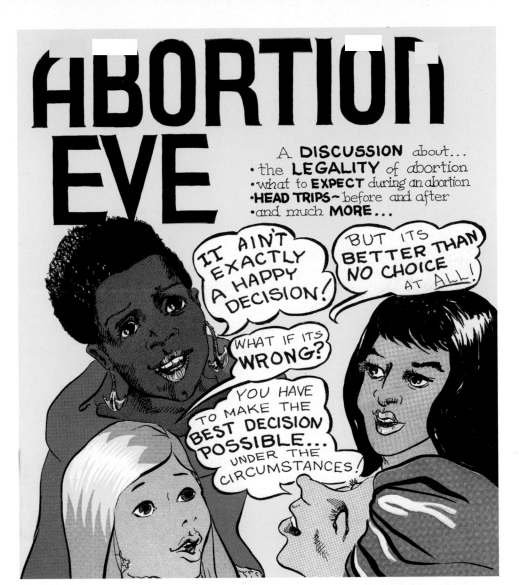

Aborton Eve was re-
leased in the wake of the
Roe v. Wade decision.

LYN CHEVLI
Underground Comix • Cartoonist

Entrepreneur and underground comix creator **Lyn Chevli (a.k.a. Chin Lyvely) combated sexism in the underground and ignorance in the mainstream.** As a co-founder of Nanny Goat Productions, she helped create the all-women comix series *Tits & Clits* and reproductive rights one-shot *Abortion Eve*.

In a time when women's health was something discussed behind closed doors, the co-founder of Nanny Goat Productions would use the comix medium to cast light on many important issues women faced in the 1970s, from the governmental regulation of women's bodies to the perception propagated by comics (and comix) created by men that the feminine body was an object of sex. As Paul Lopes writes in his book *Demanding Respect*, Chevli and Farmer "were the first to open up the comic field to female artists with a feminist perspective on everyday life, sexuality, and the crucial political issues confronting women at the time" (2009).

Chevli admired the works of fellow underground artists like R. Crumb and S. Clay Wilson, but their books didn't speak to her as a woman. Instead of waiting for someone else to make the books she was interested in, though, the sculptor and bookstore owner took matters into her own hands by fighting for feminism in comix. Out of that initiative came *Tits & Clits*—an all-female anthology that ran from 1972 to 1987.

Preceding *Wimmen's Comix* to stores by two months, Chevli and Farmer's idea to tell women's stories through women's eyes was truly original and, shortly after its publication, controversial. Chevli and Farmer found themselves on the wrong side of public perceptions about the landmark 1973 Supreme Court decision in *Miller v. California*, which established the test for determining whether material was obscene. Chevli and Farmer's work was openly labeled pornographic and obscene, proving a hindrance to distribution despite the fact that the work would have passed the Miller test for obscenity.

In 1973, the new owners of Chevli's old bookstore, Fahrenheit 451, were arrested for distributing pornographic materials, demonstrating just how closely the scrutiny impacted Chevli and her work. From an interview with *Cultural Correspondence* (Robbins 2013):

> Neither of us was much of a comics fan, but at the time we started I owned a bookstore, sold [undergrounds], and was impressed by their honesty but loathed their macho depiction of sex. Our work, originally, was a reaction to the glut of testosterone in comics... As most of us know, sex is a very political business. All we want to do is equalize that by telling our side... Our original commitment was to concentrate on female sexuality.

In response to the 1973 *Roe v. Wade* decision, Chevli and Farmer produced the one-shot comic *Abortion Eve*. As pregnancy counselors at a free clinic, Chevli and Farmer had seen first-hand the difficulties that women went through when it came to making decisions about their bodies. With *Abortion Eve*, Chevli and Farmer used the experiences of five multi-racial women to discuss the choices and issues women faced with regard to abortion. Instead of sitting on the sidelines while yet another war was waged against women, Chevli wanted to make sure that women had a place for their interests, despite (or perhaps because of) the fact that many had labeled such conversations "pornographic" and "obscene."

FURTHER READING

The Complete Wimmen's Comix edited by Trina Robbins (Fantagraphics, 2016)

Detail from Joyce Farmer's cover for *Tits & Clits* #2.

JOYCE FARMER
Underground Comix • Cartoonist

Starting in the early 1970s, Joyce Farmer was involved in two groundbreaking underground comix that countered the male-dominated field. The first, published in

partnership with Lyn Chevli in 1972, was *Tits & Clits*—also known in *The New York Times* as "a notorious series about women's sexuality whose title can't be reproduced here" (Wolk 2010). It was a response to other underground titles like *Zap Comix*, which Farmer described as "really brutal against women" (Dueben 2010). *Tits & Clits*, on the other hand, was from the perspective of "women and how they actually look at sex: they're worried about birth control, they're worried about menstrual factors. There's many factors to sex that men don't pay any attention to, and women have to pay exquisite attention to, or we pay heavily" (Campbell 2011).

In 1973, shortly after the Supreme Court's *Roe v. Wade* decision guaranteed women the right to abortion, Farmer and Chevli created the one-shot comic *Abortion Eve*. Both were then working as pregnancy counselors and wanted to help dispel abortion myths and provide matter-of-fact information about the procedure. Inside is the story of five women of different ages, races, and backgrounds who meet in the waiting room of an abortion clinic and slowly realize that their own opinions about why other women choose abortion are often wrong, and above all, irrelevant.

Farmer was also a regular contributor to another all-women underground anthology, *Wimmen's Comix*, but in the post-*Tits & Clits* years of the late 1980s and early 1990s, Farmer took an extended break from comics as she struggled to make ends meet financially. Meanwhile, her life was also consumed with caring for her aging father and stepmother. A few years after they died respectively of lung cancer and Alzheimer's, Farmer re-alized that the aging process and death were topics ripe for exploration in the graphic novel format and set about creating her tour de force *Special Exits*.

Farmer painstakingly drew, lettered, and inked all 200 pages of *Special Exits* by hand, a process that wound up taking 13 years. The result is a meticulously detailed and brutally honest memoir that does not shy away from the ugly facts of death. After *Special Exits* was published to universal critical praise, Farmer was asked in a 2010 interview with *Comic Book Resources*' Alex Dueben what she planned to do next. After so long away from the scene, perhaps a collected edition of *Tits & Clits* was in order? She admitted she wasn't sure:

> I haven't been in the comics community for years. Part of the reason why is that *Tits & Clits* was so poorly misunderstood when we did it. I got enough negative flack from enough people that I just went on with my life and didn't worry about it. If something happens now it'll be nice.

In any case, if she did choose to throw herself into another sequential art project, Farmer is sure to break more taboos. In an interview with *The Los Angeles Times*' Deborah Vankin (2010), Farmer relished this role: "I can be wild. I'm always doing something. And I don't care if it's radical or not. That's part of being an artist. You have to have an edge, or there's no point."

FURTHER READING

Special Exits by Joyce Farmer (Fantagraphics, 2010)

The Complete Wimmen's Comix edited by Trina Robbins (Fantagraphics, 2016)

Shary Flenniken's artwork for the cover of *Wimmen's Comix* #6.
(Published July 1976. Courtesy Fantagraphics.)

SHARY FLENNIKEN
Underground Comix • Cartoonist

The product of a deeply conservative military household, Shary Flenniken came of age at Vietnam protests.

There, she found an artistic calling that would place her at the epicenter of two of the most subversive humor institutions in comics history.

Born in 1950 at the height of the baby boom, Flenniken's early life followed her father's career as a Rear Admiral in the United States Navy to Alaska, Panama, and Seattle. She pursued formal art education at a commercial art school in Seattle, training to produce advertisements and other commercial graphics. At an anti-war demonstration, Flenniken was drafted to produce artwork for an underground newspaper that included "cartoons advocating freedom of choice and hitchhiking." In 1970 she met cartoonists Ted Richards, Dan O'Neill, and future husband Bobby London at the Sky River Rock Festival outside of Portland, Oregon, where she was producing the festival's mimeographed newsletter. During the festival, they produced the four-page comic *Sky River Funnies*.

In 1971, Flenniken moved to San Francisco, where she lived in a warehouse with Richards, London, O'Neill, and Gary Hallgren. The group would be immortalized as the Air Pirates, the notorious underground comix collective whose antics led to a protracted legal battle with Disney that changed the face of parody law in the United States. Flenniken didn't contribute to *Air Pirates Funnies*, the comic book that led to the confrontation with Disney, instead developing her own strip, *Trots and Bonnie*.

Trots and Bonnie found a home in *National Lampoon*, where it would appear from 1972 until 1990. Emulating the style of Golden Age cartoonists, *Trots and Bonnie* simultaneously skewered and explored sexuality, politics, and counter-culture. The juxtaposition of a charming line style that evoked the innocence of an earlier era with frank, often explicit subject matter reflecting the sexually liberal culture of the 1970s allowed Flenniken to address taboo

subjects with a great deal of empathy. Flenniken went on to become an editor of *Lampoon* under P.J. O'Rourke and recruited a variety of artists to the magazine, including Mimi Pond and Rick Geary. She also co-wrote the screenplay for *National Lampoon Goes to the Movies*.

Flenniken's professional practice placed her in competitive, male-dominated counter-culture institutions where she developed a uniquely impactful voice and visual style while paving the way for others to follow. She successfully made the transition from underground comix to the mainstream humor magazines and used her work to push back at much of the institutional sexism that pervaded both milieus. Speaking to Robert Boyd at *The Comics Journal* she said:

> Mostly I want to be understood, for them to get what I'm saying. But I'll settle for any reaction. It was a big deal for me to draw naked men with their penises showing in *Lampoon*. I wanted to put [Michelangelo's] David on the cover, with girls making fun of his little weenie. I wanted an equal time thing because what men don't seem to realize is that we all have the same reaction to seeing someone of our sex naked. It makes us nervous. We compare our bodies to the ones in the picture. It's made women totally nuts. (1991)

Flenniken currently lives in Seattle, Washington, where she provides freelance illustration for outlets, including *Mad*, *Details*, and *Graphic Classics*.

FURTHER READING

The Complete Wimmen's Comix edited by Trina Robbins (Fantagraphics, 2016)

National Lampoon's Big Book of Love by various (Rugged Land, 2004)

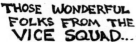

THOSE WONDERFUL FOLKS FROM THE VICE SQUAD...

IN...

bent @

"PROTECTING YER MORALS"

ONE EVENING AFTER A HEAVY DAY OF HOUSE-PAINTING, NORMA STOPS BY "THE LAVENDER LIONESS" (A YOU-KNOW-WHAT BAR!) FOR A DRINK-AND RUNS INTO AN OLD FRIEND...

KERRY! I HAVEN'T SEEN YOU IN SIX YEARS- HOW'S IT BEEN GOING?

LOTSA CHANGES, NORMA- BUT I'VE FINALLY GOTTEN MY HEAD STRAIGHTENED OUT- IF YOU'LL PARDON THE EXPRESSION-

WE'LL HAVE TO GET TOGETHER- SOON.. YOU KNOW HOW I'VE ALWAYS FELT...

I'M SO GLAD TO SEE YOU- I'LL CALL TOMORROW.

SMACK! LAVENDER LIONESS ♥

SQUEEZE

HOLD IT RIGHT THERE!

OH SHIT...

LEWD CONDUCT IN PUBLIC?!? ALL I DID WAS KISS HER!

YA HUGGED HER, TOO! BETTER GETCHER STORY STRAIGHT, HON!

FEEL FEEL

I NEVER HEARD SUCH BULLSHIT- IT WAS JUST A PLAIN OL' HUG-AN'- KISS! I DIDN'T EVEN TOUCH HER TITS, FERCHRISSAKE..!

SOB!

WE'RE GONNA GET YOU FOR USIN' OBSCENITIES IN THE PRESENCE OF A WOMAN, TOO!

Roberta Gregory took on police harassment of the LGBTQ community in this strip for *Wimmen's Comix* #7.
(Published July 1976. Courtesy Fantagraphics.)

ROBERTA GREGORY

Underground Comix • Cartoonist

Having grown up surrounded by comic books, Roberta Gregory started drawing her own comics at a very young age.

Gregory's father Bob drew and/or wrote hundreds of comics for Disney and Gold Key, most of them featuring Donald Duck. So, comics were in her blood.

The 1970s found Gregory both entering college in her native Southern California and encountering the feminist movement. As she used art and a sense of humor to explore the movement, Gregory soon found a home for her work in the influential all-women underground anthology *Wimmen's Comix* and her own *Dynamite Damsels* series. In her own words, Gregory "was happy to be living proof that feminists did have a sense of humor, but I was really just writing and drawing the sorts of stories that I would love to read, if someone else was doing them." Because no one was making the stories Gregory wanted to read, she felt obligated to make them herself.

Gregory's first *Wimmen's Comix* story appeared in issue #4. In a May 2016 interview, Gregory told the *The Beat*'s Alex Dueben about her discovery of *Wimmen's Comix*:

> I had already been drawing feminist comics for the Women's Resource Center newspaper, so I was just thrilled to see comics in real comic books that were drawn and written by women. I read comics as a child but whenever names of creators were mentioned, with the exception of Marie Severin, none of them were women's names.

Gregory became a regular contributor to *Gay Comix*, the landmark LGBTQ underground comix anthology founded by Howard Cruse. Cruse invited Gregory to submit because "They wanted to have equal representation of women and men creators and back then, I was one of the very few women doing LGBT themed stories" (Dueben 2016).

Gregory continued to publish in *Wimmen's Comix* into the 1980s, and her stories also appeared in nearly every issue of *Gay Comix*. During this period, she also started work on *Winging It*, an ambitious and intricate graphic novel that used dark humor to explore the relationship between a suicidal woman and a fallen angel, and *Sheila and the Unicorn*, a comic strip about the unrequited love between a unicorn and a human being.

In 1991, Gregory launched *Naughty Bits* and with it the character for which she is best known: Bitchy Bitch. Many related to the character, a short-tempered, profanity-spewing, middle-aged everywoman who doesn't hold back when it comes to voicing her frustrations with modern life. Bitchy appeared in 40 issues of *Naughty Bits*, which drew to a close in 2004. Gregory describes Bitchy as "the kind of person I find extremely irritating, clueless, quick to anger, no insight, and so on" (Dueben 2016).

Gregory frequently uses dark humor to explore the modern world from a feminist perspective, and her work garners a broad spectrum of reactions, from veneration to rejection. In her own words:

> I am not writing for everyone. You may absolutely hate something that I have written but you may love something else. Don't be afraid to let me know something is not your "cup of tea," (as long as you enjoy something else of mine). Believe me, I am used to it by now!

FURTHER READING

The Complete Wimmen's Comix edited by Trina Robbins (Fantagraphics, 2016)

Life's A Bitch: The Complete Bitchy Bitch Stories by Roberta Gregory (Fantagraphics, 2005)

No Straight Lines edited by Justin Hall (Fantagraphics, 2014)

Aline Kominsky-Crumb
frequently examines
beauty standards in her
work.

(Published in *Wimmen's Comix* #15, January 1989. Courtesy Fantagraphics.)

ALINE KOMINSKY-CRUMB

Underground Comix • Cartoonist

San Francisco in the 1960s and 1970s was the place to be if you were a cartoonist looking to break away from the regulations imposed on the comics industry by the Comics Code. The underground comix movement was in full force, and a truly unique voice emerged in Aline Kominsky-Crumb.

From her co-founding of *Twisted Sisters* and work as editor of the underground anthology *Weirdo* to her recent painted depictions of real women in all their modern, grotesque glory, Kominsky-Crumb has built an artistic career out of challenging gender stereotypes. Her art has been described by Peter Bagge as "artfully ugly" (1990) and *The New York Times* as "garish yet beautifully controlled" (Smith 2014), but beyond the heavily inked scrawls and bright, brassy colors, her work is infused with a sarcastic wit and knowing intelligence that has made Kominsky-Crumb an influential and powerful artist and comic creator.

Born Aline Goldsmith, Kominsky-Crumb was one of the expatriates of New York and mainstream comics who migrated to San Francisco to find a new arena for their works. A classically trained painter, Kominsky-Crumb joined Trina Robbins, Lee Marrs, and a handful of other women in founding and contributing to the longest running all-women comix anthology, *Wimmen's Comix*. Kominsky-Crumb utilized the comics form to test social boundaries, push buttons, and get in readers' faces. It was her free and unrestrained voice and style that made her not only one of the most prominent creators in the underground, but also one of the most influential creators for future alternative and independent comics.

Whereas many other women comix creators were content to reside in the gendered narrative spaces they created for themselves, Kominsky-Crumb wanted more and wasn't afraid to play dirty with the boys. "Right from the beginning I got a lot of flak from everyone for being so primitive and self-deprecating," Kominsky-Crumb recalls in an interview with Peter Bagge for *The Comics Journal*. "Women like Trina were influenced by traditional comics. They had images of women being glamorous and heroic. I didn't have that background." When she wasn't contributing to *Wimmen's Comix*, she was contributing to other underground anthologies such as Robert Crumb's *Weirdo*, collaborating on comics like *Dirty Laundry*, and in general making comics that told an entirely different story about modern women.

After falling out with the *Wimmen's Comix* collective, Kominsky-Crumb joined Diane Noomin in founding *Twisted Sisters*, which took the underground in a whole new direction. Unlike *Wimmen's Comix*, the central theme of which was the empowerment of women, *Twisted Sisters* showed women as they were, with all of their mortal flaws and desires. Noomin recalled, "Basically, we felt that our type of humor was self-deprecating and ironic and that what they were pushing for in the name of feminism and political correctness was a sort of self-aggrandizing and idealistic view of women as a super-race. We preferred to have our flaws and show them" (2004).

Kominsky-Crumb owned the "flawed" woman and used her own experiences and emotional insecurities for her gritty art and stories. Today, Kominsky-Crumb continues to write and draw stories that speak to her, from comics like *Power Pak*, to her graphic memoir *Need More Love*, to her paintings. Kominsky-Crumb has never been held back by any kind of boundary—gender, ethnic, or social—and her unabashed approach to art and comics has made her a leading voice in comics and art.

FURTHER READING

The Complete Wimmen's Comix edited by Trina Robbins (Fantagraphics, 2016)

Need More Love: A Graphic Memoir by Aline Kominsky-Crumb (MQ Publications, 2007)

Lee Marrs' "My Deadly Darling Dyke" first appeared in *Gay Comix* #5.

(Reprinted in *No Straight Lines*, Fantagraphics, 2014. Courtesy Lee Marrs and Justin Hall.)

LEE MARRS
Underground Comix • Cartoonist

Not content to just be a pioneer of the underground comix movement, Lee Marrs stands to this day as one of the most well-versed and outspoken comics creators in the industry. From being a "founding mommy" (Uyeno 2015) of *Wimmen's Comix* and creator of the beloved underground comic *Pudge, Girl Blimp* to her work for DC, Marvel, and Dark Horse, Marrs has made a career out of defying stereotypes and breaking down the proverbial boys' club.

Like many artists of the time, Marrs got her start working in the comics industry as a part-time assistant on comic strips like *Little Orphan Annie, Hi & Lois,* and *Prince Valiant.* Marrs' beginning in the industry may have been humble, but an entrepreneurial drive and ambition to create comics for herself and characters that she owned ultimately led her to San Francisco,

California—home of the underground comix movement—in the late 1960s, where she would put her own stamp on the comix industry.

Although the comix scene itself still carried elements of a boys' club mentality, that didn't stop Marrs from making the comics she wanted. Like other women in the underground, Marrs shared a passion for telling stories by, for, and about women. A meeting with Trina Robbins while she was doing work for underground newspapers would result in Marrs becoming one of the founders of *Wimmen's Comix*.

Much like the boys' club, Marrs saw past the "wimmen's club," and in 1973 she went off on her own to create her most iconic comic book series to date—*Pudge, Girl Blimp*. Following the failed sexual adventures of an overweight 17-year-old runaway from Normal, Illinois, Marrs created a story that was not only incredibly relatable but truly revolutionary. The idea of a protagonist being an overweight, horny, and admittedly unattractive teenager making her way through the hippie counterculture of San Francisco was unheard of, but fans of the underground loved it. For once, someone was telling a story to which so many young women could relate. *Pudge* would run until 1978 and has recently been collected to inspire a new generation of comics fans.

Beyond Marrs' work contributing to other underground anthologies like *Gay Comix*, *Star*Reach*, and *Heavy Metal*, she would also land work in the animation industry, where she would become an Emmy Award–winning art director. Marrs is also a shining beacon in the mainstream, working on *House of Secrets* and *Wonder Woman* for DC, "Crazy Lady" for Marvel's *Crazy*, and *Indiana Jones* and *Sexy Chix* for Dark Horse, all of which solidify her voice and presence in the industry she loves.

FURTHER READING

The Further Fattening Adventures of Pudge, Girl Blimp by Lee Marrs (Marrs Books, 2016)

The Complete Wimmen's Comix edited by Trina Robbins (Fantagraphics, 2016)

No Straight Lines edited by Justin Hall (Fantagraphics, 2014)

Marrs used comics to comment on women's traditional roles.
(From "Cyberfenetics," published in *Wimmen's Comix* #4, January 1974. Courtesy Fantagraphics.)

"...being aggressive had no meaning in a woman's life until she had the possibilities a man does...now, women will move into all areas of living— including crime."

Dr. Leon Salzman, Clinical Professor of Psychiatry at the Albert Einstein College of Medicine in New York

DIDI GLITZ
SHE CHOSE CRIME

Diane Noomin ©1974

Diane Noomin's Didi Glitz as she appeared in Wimmen's Comix #4.
(Published January 1974. Courtesy Fantagraphics.)

DIANE NOOMIN
Underground Comix • Cartoonist

An original contributor to *Wimmen's Comix*, co-founder of the equally important *Twisted Sisters*, and creator of her boisterous doppelgänger Didi Glitz, Diane Noomin was a true renegade of the underground comix scene.

The work that Noomin did early in her career (and still does today) set the groundwork for the graphic memoirs that are prevalent in the industry now. Noomin not only saw underground comix as a way to tell her own personal stories outside the boundaries set by the mainstream, but also as a mechanism for blurring gender lines within her artistic community, which she perceived at the time as becoming almost exclusive in its establishment of gendered collectives.

Unlike some female comix creators of the 1970s, who were paving the way for women through the creation of all-female comic collectives, Noomin saw the artistic value in blending her talents and telling her stories in the same books as underground legends like R. Crumb, Bill Griffith, and Art Spiegelman. For Noomin, the possibility and power of the medium, especially for women, extended past a starkly defined male/female divide, and it is in this space that she conquered and explicitly proved that the proverbial boys' club was indeed no girls' club, either.

"There was a very strong need for feminism across the board in this country," said Noomin in an interview with *The Comics Journal*. "That wasn't my interest in doing comics. My interest was in personal stories" (Rudick 2012). For Noomin, her response to this female call-to-action wasn't to segregate herself or to help establish girls' clubs. Rather, she saw the awareness of the feminist cause as an opportunity to do something different for women's comics and women creators: taking advantage of the larger underground comix movement and its perceived men-only spaces to insert herself into those narratives. Whether it be *Weirdo*, *Young Lust*, *Arcade*, or *Wimmen's Comix*—all books to which Noomin contributed—the important thing for Noomin was the story, but not the story as it could be told within the confines of gender politics.

"I could do comics about anything!" notes Noomin (Rudick 2012). If she couldn't find the right space to tell her own story, Noomin created it, and that was how *Twisted Sisters* was born in 1976. When Aline Kominsky-Crumb and

Noomin felt that the women's collective mentality was becoming more about politics—"a hot-bed of bickering and power plays" (Noomin 2004)—and less about telling women's stories, they got in touch with publisher Last Gasp and "just created our own comic" (Rudick 2012).

For Noomin and Kominsky-Crumb, "we preferred to have our flaws and show them" (Noomin 2004). *Twisted Sisters* would become a unique and revolutionary publication in that it was a series about women and their stories, but it operated outside the comics spaces fashioned by women creators. It put women in touch with men and celebrated the dirty and flawed aspects of their persons within a broader and more complicated world not protected by feminism.

Out of this reactionary approach to feminist comics, the sassy Didi Glitz was born. "Equal parts sex, anxiety, domesticity, and rebellion—by turns a garish, boozy mess and a modern, self-affirming woman" (Rudick 2004), Didi epitomized what Noomin was trying to accomplish with *Twisted Sisters* and her exodus from *Wimmen's Comix*. Didi would become Noomin's comic doppelgänger and a vehicle to tell stories and share experiences that were more personal and autobiographical. Noomin's subject matter may have been "the woman," but her storytelling was about showing her raw, human side.

FURTHER READING

The Complete Wimmen's Comix edited by Trina Robbins (Fantagraphics, 2016)

Glitz-2-Go by Diane Noomin (Fantagraphics, 2012)

TRINA ROBBINS

Underground Comix • Cartoonist & Historian

One of comics' most influential creators and historians, Trina Robbins has spent her career as the preeminent advocate for women's place in the industry. Her stories, historical books, and lectures set the standard for the appreciation of women's contributions to the field.

Robbins rose from science fiction fandom in the 1950s to become a part of underground and magazine comics in the late 1960s. In 1969, she contributed to the New York underground newspaper *The East Village Other* and its comix spin-off *Gotham Blimp Works*. She also co-created Vampirella for Warren Publishing with fandom icon Forrest J. Ackerman, providing the character with her iconic visual elements. In 1970, Robbins moved to San Francisco, where she quickly became a participant in the city's freewheeling youth counterculture and developed her feminist approach to comics.

In a time when the only path to unfettered expression in comics came from working outside of the confines of the Comics Code, Robbins devoted herself to creating and editing underground comix. In 1970, she produced the first-ever all-women comic, *It Ain't Me, Babe*, with Willy Mendes and Lisa Lyons. This inspired her co-founding of *Wimmen's Comix*, and Robbins contributed to the series throughout its 20-year run. Robbins' own comics continued during this period, with the solo *Trina's Women* from Kitchen Sink, plus contributions to nationally-circulated magazines such as *National Lampoon* and *High Times*, and undergrounds, including *Barbarian Comics*, *San Francisco Comic Book*, *Snarf*, *Yellow Dog*, and *Wet Satin*.

From the 1980s onward, Robbins expanded her output into mainstream comics, contributing to titles for Marvel and DC, most notably *The Legend of Wonder Woman* with Kurt Busiek, and the domestic abuse–themed *Wonder Woman: The Once & Future Story* with Colleen Doran. In 2000, she created the all-ages superhero series *Go Girl!* with Anne Timmons, which was published by Image and Dark Horse. Simultaneously, she was also continuing her work as an activist and editor, using comics to address the AIDS crisis, abortion rights, and other social issues.

More than a prolific creative voice, Robbins is also one of the industry's most prominent authors and archivists of the complex role that women creators have played in comics since their inception. Robbins describes herself as not only a writer, but a "herstorian" whose books include the surveys *Pretty in Ink*, *The Great Women Cartoonists*, *The Great*

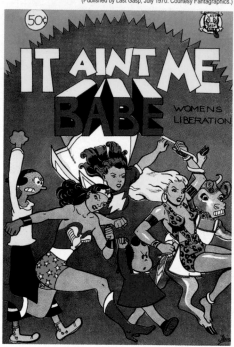

It Ain't Me, Babe was the first all-women anthology.
(Published by Last Gasp, July 1970. Courtesy Fantagraphics.)

Women Superheroes, and *From Girls to Grrlz*, as well as the biographical presentations *Lily Renée, Escape Artist*, and *The Brinkley Girls*. Robbins opened the door for a new generation of comics fans and readers to enjoy and celebrate the fantastically rich history that women have in this industry by collecting materials and presenting viewpoints that have never before been seen.

FURTHER READING

The Complete Wimmen's Comix edited by Trina Robbins (Fantagraphics, 2016)

Pretty In Ink: North American Women Cartoonists 1896–2013 by Trina Robbins (Fantagraphics, 2013)

Lily Renée, Escape Artist by Trina Robbins, Anne Timmons, and Mo Oh (Graphic Universe, 2011)

DORI SEDA
Underground Comix • Cartoonist

The comics of Dori Seda portray her determination to do the patient work of chronicling a fun life lived against the grain. Born in 1951 and encouraged from an early age to become an artist, Seda pursued formal art education at Illinois State University, where she achieved a B.A. in art for painting and ceramics. Her ceramic works reveal the wry and ribald wit that would characterize her later comics.

After college, Seda moved to San Francisco, where she became a fixture in the Mission District art and bar scenes. In 1979 she went to work at Last Gasp, the venerable underground publisher and distributor, starting as a janitor and moving up to bookkeeper. Seda kept night hours, in part due to her own nocturnal rhythms and in part to mitigate the jealousy she felt when interacting with the cartoonists who thought of her solely as "the bookkeeper." Seda's fortunes changed when R. Crumb accepted her 1977 story "Bloods in Space" for *Weirdo* #2. Crumb encouraged Seda and provided a regular berth in the anthology from 1982 until 1985.

Seda found her calling in comics. Her largely autobiographical work portrays the rude, sleazy, anything-goes sexuality of pre-AIDS San Francisco with equal parts bleak humor and cheerful enjoyment. Her work depicts sexuality in a way that emphasizes feminine pleasure, power, and above all else, agency. In the context of her irreverent and explicit drawings, her 1986 solo title *Lonely*

Seda's artwork from the back cover of *Wimmen's Comix* #9.
(Published May 1984. Courtesy Fantagraphics.)

Nights Comics was banned in the UK. Her 1987 story "How Cops 'Pick Up' Girls" protested the sexual harassment and abuse of power she experienced at the hands of the SFPD. "Door of Deception, or The Right to Lie," a collaboration with Carla Abbots, exposed the tactics of anti-abortion clinics. "The Do-Nothing Decade" examined political apathy.

Seda suffered from the respiratory disease silicosis, which was made worse by her hard living. On February 25, 1988, Seda died of flu-induced respiratory failure at the warehouse she shared with Don Donahue. Seda's mother inherited the rights to her work and sought to suppress it on moral grounds. A 1987 letter written six days after Seda's 36th birthday saved her work from oblivion. Cartoonist Leslie Sternbergh recalls:

> "TO WHOM IT MAY CONCERN," the letter begins. "This is sort of a contract and sort of a will (although I don't plan on dying soon.)" ... She makes one point clearly—and several times reiterates it—that Don [Donahue] should have her artwork... This odd contract was at her insistence witnessed by her friends Krystine Kryttre and Dan O'Neill. For whatever reasons, she wanted a legal document. (Seda 1999)

In 1990, with the assistance of Last Gasp founder Ron Turner and attorney Mitch Berger, the process of filing the letter as Seda's will began. Donahue took ownership of Seda's work in 1991, protecting her legacy.

FURTHER READING

The Complete Wimmen's Comix edited by Trina Robbins (Fantagraphics, 2016)

Dori Stories: The Complete Dori Seda by Dori Seda (Last Gasp, 1999)

Jessica Abel first worked in self-published zines.

JESSICA ABEL
Alternative Comics • Cartoonist

In the 1990s, artist Jessica Abel would find her voice in one of the remaining vestiges of underground comix—the zine. She would also become a true pioneer of the genre that we now embrace as alternative comics and someone dedicated to bringing comics into school curricula.

The award-winning artist got her start in comics in 1992 by photocopying and hand-sewing individual issues of her zine *Art Babe*. A series of individual non-fiction stories about native Chicagoans like herself, these hand-crafted, self-published comics were the roots of what would become standard fare at the Small Press Expo (SPX) and Alternative Press Expo (APE).

Abel embraced the autobiographical narrative form and used comics not only as a means to tell her story—and by extension the stories of those like her—but also to comment upon the medium itself. Focusing on the lives of those in modern urban settings, Abel chronicled city life and the young creative people who called Chicago home. "She's a literary cartoonist, chronicling a free-floating crowd of young, hip, pleasure-seeking barhoppers who also double as art students, wannabe writers, rock musicians and low-wage clerical workers," writes *Publishers Weekly* about Abel's *Art Babe* collection. Abel's characters may be young and inexperienced, but her introspective storytelling gets to the heart of their relationships and liaisons. "Abel's female characters project both a sense of unfettered social audacity as well as a capacity for neurotic self-absorption, a fictional profile of Abel's own go-getting, post-feminist generation" (*Publishers Weekly*).

In 1995, she would be awarded the prestigious Xeric Award, which made it possible for her to complete *Art Babe #5* and to ultimately collect the series in a single volume. From that point forward, Abel would become one of the biggest voices of the alternative comics scene. Since *Art Babe*, the self-proclaimed "super narrative geek" has continued to hone her craft. From writing about a young woman's attempt to find herself in Mexico City (*La Perdida*), to a book about the masters of radio (*Out on the Wire*), to the story of a hoverderby player on Mars (*Trish Trash: Rollergirl of Mars*), Abel embraces the unique narrative power of comics. "In a lot of ways, my story is all about investigating story," says Abel. "I love finding systems, strategies, and tools that allow me to make the strongest stories possible. It helps that I'm intense and long-sighted, with a gift for understanding deep narrative structure." (Abel 2016)

Although Abel has spent decades telling her own story, she has also dedicated the past several years to educating others and helping them find their own narrative voices. From teaching at the School of Visual Arts, to organizing comics workshops, to making books that are dedicated to mastering the craft of comics, Abel has been a pioneer of comics in the classroom and a strong advocate for comics as an outlet for free expression. Abel may have started with self-published zines, but she has influenced the way that so many new creators tell their personal stories today. Her decades of pounding the pavement have opened new doors both within and outside the comics industry.

FURTHER READING

La Perdida by Jessica Abel (Pantheon, 2008)

Out on the Wire: The Storytelling Secrets of the New Masters of Radio by Jessica Abel (Broadway Books, 2015)

Trish Trash #1: Rollergirl of Mars by Jessica Abel (Super Genius, 2016)

Barry examined the demons that plague creators in *One! Hundred! Demons!*
(© Lynda Barry. Courtesy Drawn & Quarterly.)

LYNDA BARRY
Alternative Comics • Cartoonist

Born Linda Jean Barry, cartoonist Lynda Barry is one of alternative comics' most celebrated creators.

Known not only for her strip work in alternative weeklies, Barry is also acclaimed for her incredible autobiographical works, which capture highly personal and introspective aspects of her life in a way that diverse audiences can appreciate. A pioneer of the biographical and experimental comics form, Barry opened the door for many of the themes and styles that have found a place in alternative comics today.

Born in Wisconsin in 1956, Barry's family moved to Seattle, Washington, shortly thereafter. She credits comic strips with helping her learn how to read, and a chance encounter with R. Crumb's *Zap* in junior high helped Barry recognize that "you could write about anything" in comics (Powers 1989). While attending Evergreen State College in Olympia, Washington, Barry began her first foray into comics in 1977 with the publication of *Ernie Pook's Comeek* in the school paper. Shortly after graduating, she returned to Seattle, but she didn't intend to make a career of comics until her friend Matt Groening pitched her work to *Chicago Reader*'s Bob Roth. Barry refers to it as "sheer luck" (Powers 1989), but publication in *Chicago Reader* meant her work found a home in alternative weeklies around the country.

Barry may be best known for *Ernie Pook's Comeek*, which ran in alternative weeklies from the 1970s to the 1990s. With *Ernie Pook's Comeek*, Barry was able to reach out to a new comics reader, one who was looking for more complex and challenging works than those that were being written for the daily newspaper. Ostensibly the story of two regular sisters, Marlys and Arna, the comic was in a sense everyone's story. Barry's honest narrative coupled with her unique art style captured the lives of ordinary people in an authentic way that was never forced or over-taxed. "Cartoonist Lynda Barry brought tremendous empathy and a finely tuned sense of interior life to *Ernie Pook's Comeek*," writes *Isthmus*, one of the papers that ran the comic strip (2012).

In contrast to the underground comix scenes, which remained fairly isolated to a particular community and its creators, Barry was syndicated across North America in various alternative weeklies. Barry's work reached all sorts of people and places. As her popularity grew and alternative weeklies and comics changed, Barry would also diversify, becoming not only a comics creator, but an illustrator, writer, playwright, and teacher. She experimented with different media as a means to get her voice and story to new audiences. Doing so meant adapting her illustrated novel *The Good Times are Killing Me* into an award-winning off-Broadway play or creating what she calls "autobifictionalography" (Arnold 2002) by delving into her innermost spaces in *One! Hundred! Demons!* Thus, Barry's work reached a variety of audiences and ultimately inspired other contemporary comics creators and artists.

In 2009 Barry won both a prestigious Eisner Award and the R.R. Donnelly Award—Wisconsin's highest literary achievement—for her graphic novel *What It Is*. A memoir, a graphic novel, and an instructional workbook for a new generation of comics creators, *What It Is* "offers us insight into how [Barry] overcame self-doubt, as well as the doubts of others, to follow her muse, and in the process become one of America's leading cartoonists" (Strand 2009).

Throughout her career, Barry has never once settled for a single form of expression. In an interview with Amazon after the release of *Picture This* (Drawn & Quarterly 2010), Barry spoke to her goals as a creator:

> My goal is to make a book for someone who is sitting in the waiting room at the Jiffy Lube while they were getting their oil changed. I want to make books that are picked up by a bored or waiting person who starts to thumb through them and gets drawn in enough so that they stop noticing they are waiting at the Jiffy Lube and instead start to itch to make something with their hands. A picture, or a comic or anything at all. I'm devoted to the idea that the use of images can not only transform our experience of time and space, but also has an absolute biological function that is directly tied to an essential state of being which is this: the feeling that life is something worth living.

FURTHER READING

What It Is by Lynda Barry (Drawn & Quarterly, 2008)

One! Hundred! Demons! by Lynda Barry (Drawn & Quarterly, 2005)

Syllabus: Notes from an Accidental Professor by Lynda Barry (Drawn & Quarterly, 2014)

Kate Beaton frequently examines the work of historical women, in this case scientist Rosalind Franklin.
(Courtesy Kate Beaton.)

KATE BEATON
Alternative Comics • Cartoonist

As a self-taught comic creator from the first generation to come of age on the Internet, Kate Beaton first shared her comics online simply as a way to stay in touch with distant friends. Before long this placed her among the pantheon of webcomics pioneers, but her sustained success in the years since is entirely due to her unique facility for comic timing, facial expressions, and historical humor that is both zany and erudite.

Beaton was born in 1983 in the tiny coastal village of Mabou, Nova Scotia. Growing up in the tight-knit rural community, she was recognized early on as one of a few students in her class of 23 who could draw. With no art classes offered at the local K–12 school, Beaton's parents cultivated her natural talent by getting her involved in 4-H and by introducing her to local artists. In those days her exposure to comics was mostly through the strips that happened to run in the newspaper, the *Foxtrot* collections which she bought at school book fairs, and the old *Peanuts* books in the school library.

While attending Mount Allison University, where Beaton majored in history and anthropology, she submitted comics to the student newspaper and eventually became editor of the comics section. She relished the chance to flex her creative muscles and to finally get informed feedback for her work.

After college, though, Beaton again found herself without an audience. To pay off her student loan, she did soul-deadening office work. To cheer herself up in the evenings, she worked on pencil-and-ink comics and, encouraged by friends, uploaded them to LiveJournal and then-nascent Facebook.

In short order, Beaton's work had begun to pivot toward what she is most known for today: quirky but informative spoofs of historic figures and classic literature. She soon amassed a devoted following, and was surprised to find herself at the vanguard of a new format: webcomics. In 2008 she moved her work to her own website, *Hark! A Vagrant*, and took the plunge of working on comics full time.

In 2009 Beaton self-published her first book, *Never Learn Anything From History*, and was more than a little embarrassed when her signing line at SPX dwarfed those of more established creators. She also became an unwilling symbol of the alleged battle between webcomics and print, as she told *The Comics Journal*'s Chris Mautner during a 2015 interview:

When I came in it was "Print vs. Web! Who's cool and who's legit and who's not or who deserves what." I never had

invested in any part of comics culture at all. So it was like coming in and looking into the glass window and seeing all this kerfuffle that I just watched it with interest. I didn't identify with either side.

Beaton's blockbuster success continued with her next book, *Hark! A Vagrant*, (Drawn & Quarterly, 2011). *Time* critic Lev Grossman described it as "the wittiest book of the year" (2011), while *The Globe and Mail*'s Martin Levin said it was "one of the most innovative and delightful collections I've come across" (Medley 2015). The book spent five months on *The New York Times* bestseller list and made more than 20 best-of lists, and Beaton won a total of four Harvey Awards in 2011 and 2012.

During this time, Beaton lived in Brooklyn and Toronto, also ticking off a long-time goal of having some cartoons published in *The New Yorker*. For her 2015 collection, *Step Aside, Pops,* Drawn & Quarterly ordered its largest-ever first printing of 50,000 copies. The book spent six months on *The New York Times* bestseller list and made more than 25 best-of lists. In 2015, Beaton also broke into children's books with *The Princess and the Pony* (Scholastic), the tale of a young warrior princess and her flatulent pony. Beaton continues to post historical comics online at *Hark! A Vagrant*.

FURTHER READING

Hark! A Vagrant by Kate Beaton (Drawn & Quarterly, 2011)

Step Aside, Pops: A Hark! A Vagrant Collection by Kate Beaton (Drawn & Quarterly, 2015)

The Princess and the Pony by Kate Beaton (Arthur A. Levine Books, 2015)

MY FATHER ONCE NEARLY CAME TO BLOWS WITH A FEMALE DINNER GUEST ABOUT WHETHER A PARTICULAR PATCH OF EMBROIDERY WAS FUCHSIA OR MAGENTA.

BUT THE INFINITE GRADATIONS OF COLOR IN A FINE SUNSET--FROM SALMON TO CANARY TO MIDNIGHT BLUE--LEFT HIM WORDLESS.

This panel from p. 150 of *Fun Home* displays Bechdel's talent for characterization.

(© 2006 Alison Bechdel. Courtesy Houghton Mifflin Harcourt.)

ALISON BECHDEL

Alternative Comics • Cartoonist

Alison Bechdel has led the way in bringing **LGBTQ comics and graphic memoir from the pages of alt-weeklies to mainstream bookstores, library shelves, and classrooms.** From her long-running cult favorite strip *Dykes to Watch Out For* to her pair of memoirs *Fun Home* and *Are You My Mother?*, Bechdel exhibits unmatched skill in rendering character interactions with wry humor and keen perception.

Bechdel grew up in the small town of Beech Creek, Pennsylvania, the daughter of high school English teachers. Her family also owned and lived in the local funeral home, which her father Bruce meticulously restored in his spare time. When Bechdel reached young adulthood and realized she was a lesbian, her mother informed her of a fact that made many puzzle pieces from her childhood fall into place: Bruce was also gay and may have had liaisons with underage students. Just a few weeks after Bechdel told her parents of her sexuality, Bruce was struck and killed by a car while restoring another house. His death was ruled an accident.

Bechdel began her now-legendary comic strip *Dykes to Watch Out For* in 1983 at the urging of friends who were amused by the cartoon doodles that adorned the margins of her letters. Within a few years, the strip, which explored the various archetypes of lesbian subculture, was syndicated in alternative publications across the country. *A Dykes to Watch Out For* strip entitled "The Rule" also established what has come to be known as the Bechdel test, which gauges the meaningful character development of women in movies and other pop culture. To successfully pass the test, a piece must feature at least two women talking to each about something other than a man.

Bechdel's 2006 graphic novel *Fun Home*, which recounts her complicated relationship with her father, met with widespread critical praise and mainstream success, which also led to it being challenged in several locations. In 2006 it was temporarily removed from the public library in Marshall, Missouri, after a patron said it was pornographic, but the book was returned to shelves after the library drafted a collection development policy to protect controversial material that was also critically acclaimed and/or in demand. In 2008, a challenge at the University of Utah was also shut down when the English department and the university affirmed that the single student who objected to the book had been reasonably accommodated with an alternate assignment.

In 2014, *Fun Home* faced a greater challenge in South Carolina, where some state legislators proposed punitive budget cuts against the College of Charleston because it incorporated the book into a voluntary summer reading program for incoming freshman. After months of debate, the legislature reached an unsatisfactory but highly ironic "compromise": the funding would be restored, but it would be used for teaching about historic documents, including the Constitution. *Fun Home* was also one of the books a 20-year-old student and her parents wanted eradicated from the curriculum at a California community college. This 2015 attempt to censor the book failed as well.

Despite the controversy, Bechdel was awarded a MacArthur Foundation "genius grant" in 2014. Further, the musical version of *Fun Home* has garnered critical acclaim and won the Pulitzer.

FURTHER READING

Fun Home: A Family Tragicomic by Alison Bechdel (Houghton Mifflin Harcourt, 2006)

Are You My Mother?: A Comic Drama by Alison Bechdel (Houghton Mifflin Harcourt, 2012)

The Essential Dykes to Watch Out For by Alison Bechdel (Houghton Mifflin Harcourt, 2008)

Where I'm Coming From by Barbara Brandon-Croft may have ended in 2005, but the strips still ring true today.

BARBARA BRANDON-CROFT

Daily Comics • Syndicated Cartoonist

The first Black woman to publish a nationally syndicated comic strip, Barbara Brandon-Croft does not get nearly the recognition she deserves.

Years before Aaron McGruder's *The Boondocks* became one of the most recognizably Black comic strips with important political commentary, Brandon-Croft's *Where I'm Coming From* reclaimed the funnies as a space where Black women's voices could be represented and amplified.

The daughter of Brumsic Brandon Jr., a cartoonist made famous by his strip *Luther*, Brandon-Croft's big break arrived when she published the first *Where I'm Coming From* strips in the *Detroit Free Press*. Two years later she signed a contract with Universal Press Syndicate. Eventually "the girls," as Brandon-Croft referred to her characters, would not only span over 100 U.S. cities, but also stretch across the diaspora by appearing in Jamaican and South African publications as well.

Brandon-Croft had two missions with *Where I'm Coming From.* First, she wanted White readers to fully grasp the struggles of Black Americans as people in their own right, not just characters that happened to be brown-skinned. As she explained in an interview with *The New York Times,* "If mainstream folk understood the Black perspective better, they wouldn't be surprised at the rage we're holding. We know White people because we're exposed to them, but they don't know us. If we're going to have a peaceful existence, they have to understand our perspective" (Rule 1992).

Arguably more important was the second part of Brandon-Croft's mission, which was to speak on politically-charged issues through characters with whom Black women readers could readily identify. Brandon-Croft claims that the simplistic style of the strip was instrumental in achieving this, since Black women "are too often summed up by our body parts" and tend to be viewed as "at the bottom of the totem pole," adding that her work sought to communicate that Black women "'have opinions,' and 'Look me in the eye and talk to me,'" (Rule 1992). From rape convictions, to "don't ask, don't tell," to the challenges of being a single mother, Brandon-Croft's characters showcased a depth of feeling and sharpness of intellect that media representations of Black women so desperately needed.

Sadly, the following for *Where I'm Coming From* dwindled before the end of its 14-year run in 2005, but Brandon-Croft continues to marry her artistic talent with strong activism. Her most recent contributions include illustrations for a guide for Black teen girls by Franchestra Ahmen-Cawthorne, entitled *Sista Girlfren Breaks It Down...: When Mom's Not Around,* and the anthology *APB: Artists Against Police Brutality.*

FURTHER READING

APB: Artists Against Police Brutality edited by Bill Campbell, Jason Rodriguez, and John Jennings (Rosarium Publishing, 2015)

Brandon-Croft frequently addressed police brutality in her work.
(© Barbara Brandon-Croft. Dated April 6, 2000. Courtesy Barbara Brandon-Croft.)

CLAIRE BRETÉCHER

Alternative Comics • Cartoonist

Her comics career began in the early 1960s, a few years before Claire Bretécher's native France would be roiled by social upheaval and a sharp left turn in politics. From the midst of the earnest radical movement, Bretécher lovingly cataloged the foibles of her compatriots, earning a place in the pantheon of French comics. "Two things distinguished her presence on the page: a total independence and a personal audacity," explains Cynthia Rose in a 2016 article for *The Comics Journal.*

Claire Bretécher grew up in Nantes, France, but left for Paris as soon as she reached adulthood. Although her background was in fine arts, she abandoned that pursuit upon finding that comics—her first love—were "persona non grata" in highbrow art. After a few years contributing illustrations to various magazines, she made her big break into the industry by drawing the René Goscinny–authored series *Facteur Rhésus* in 1963. Throughout the rest of the 1960s, she contributed mostly to three comic magazines that were then in their heyday: *Spirou*, *Pilote*, and *Tintin* (which prominently featured

Hergé's boy reporter but also included other series).

In 1969 Bretécher created one of her most well-known characters: Cellulite, a quasi-medieval princess and acerbic feminist. A few years later Bretécher was one of the founders of the adult-oriented comic magazine *L'Écho des Savanes*, but she left in 1973 for a regular spot in the news weekly *Le Nouvel Observateur*, where she set about dissecting French society in a comic that became known as *La Page des Frustrés*. There, she gained admirers such as the cultural critic Roland Barthes, who dubbed her "the best sociologist of the year" in 1976 (*Lambiek Comiclopedia* 2014).

Few of Bretécher's comics have been translated into English. In 1978, *National Lampoon* collected some of Bretécher's *Les Frustrés* strips into an English-language edition, and a review in *The Comics Journal* called her work "probably the most palatable Gallic import since champagne" (Thompson 1978). In her introduction to the collection, Bretécher noted that "Women understand my cartoons better than men do. I don't mind giving feminists a hard time, probably because I'm squarely on their side."

In the 1980s Bretécher self-published several albums, including a controversially irreverent comic biography of Saint Theresa of Avila. Then in 1988 she created another character that became a well-loved French icon: Agrippine, the quintessentially dissatisfied teenager and rebellious daughter of aging leftists.

Through Cellulite and Agrippine, Bretécher lovingly skewered what she considered to be the excesses of two causes she nonetheless believed in: feminism and the leftist movement that flowered in May 1968 but leaves its mark on French society to this day. Bretécher has retired from comics, but her enduring influence is evident in France and beyond—from the licensed Agrippine merchandise that proliferates in European novelty shops to the asteroid that received her name in 2006. "She is a virtuoso and a national treasure, an artist whose work explodes with style, wit—and creative complaining," explains Rose (2016).

FURTHER READING

Agrippina (multiple volumes; French: *Agrippine*) by Claire Bretécher (Europe Comics)

Agrippina explores the relationships among four generations of women.
(From *Agrippina and the Ancestor*. ©2016 Claire Bretécher. Courtesy Europe Comics.)

#1 NEW YORK TIMES BESTSELLER

Can't we talk about something more PLEASANT?

ROZ CHAST
A MEMOIR

Roz Chast's *Can't We Talk About Something More Pleasant?* skillfully merges grief and humor.

ROZ CHAST
Alternative Comics • Cartoonist

Since 1978 Rosalind "Roz" Chast's cartoons have graced the pages of *The New Yorker* along with numerous other publications. Called "the magazine's only certifiable genius" by editor David Remnick, the award-winning cartoonist, author, and children's book illustrator has made a career out of depicting the raw and real aspects of her own life and, by extension, ours. From *Theories of Everything* and *The Alphabet from A to Y with Bonus Letter Z!* to her graphic memoir *Can't We Talk About Something More Pleasant?*, Chast has mastered the craft of balancing comedy with reality, and she has dominated the highly competitive professional field of editorial cartoons.

Having a fondness for drawing from an early age, Chast studied art at the Rhode Island School of Design, but she chose to major in painting because cartooning, especially to make people laugh, "was very bad in art school during the mid-seventies" (Gehr 2011). After graduating, she returned to her native New York, never expecting to get a job in cartooning. In 1978, while still living at home with her parents, Chast left a packet of cartoons at *The New Yorker* offices for review. Despite feeling that her work didn't fit at the magazine, she ended up selling a piece and was invited to submit regularly.

As she delved into editorial cartooning, Chast faced the same obstacles that many young women did during that time. When asked whether her gender was an issue, Chast explained:

To some extent, yeah. I've been very fortunate to have had editors who, even if they were guys, didn't always go for jackass-type humor. But when I first walked into that room, it was all men. And it wasn't just that it was guys, it was that they were all older. Being female at *The New Yorker* was just one of many things. I also had a different sensibility, I was a lot younger, and I probably didn't want to be there. I wanted to be there, but for me it was just very…fraught. I was shy. I didn't know how to talk to anybody. (Gehr 2014)

Chast saw art and humor as a way to make sense of mortality and sorrow, and it is that humorous and honest approach to topics like life, death, and the ordinary and mundane that have made her a voice that resonates with so many people. "I've done a lot of death cartoons—tombstones, Grim Reaper, illness, obituaries…" said the cartoonist in an interview with *Forbes* magazine. "I'm not great at analyzing things, but my guess is that maybe the only relief from the terror of being alive is jokes" (Donnelly 2014).

Her greatest and most personal work to date is the memoir *Can't We Talk About Something More Pleasant?* Tackling the difficult subject of death by telling the story of her parents' last years alive, Chast shares one of the saddest parts of being human through a lens of humor, building a truly unique narrative not many can emulate. The book was a finalist for the 2014 National Book Award in nonfiction. "I think that this is something that—at least from the mail that I've gotten—people are going through or have gone through similar things, taking care of extremely elderly parents," said Chast in an interview with the National Book Foundation.

FURTHER READING

Can't We Talk about Something More Pleasant? by Roz Chast (Bloomsbury, 2014)

Theories of Everything: Selected, Collected, and Health-Inspected Cartoons, 1978–2006 by Roz Chast (Bloomsbury, 2008)

The Party, After You Left by Roz Chast (Bloomsbury, 2014)

In "State Violence," Coe
takes on injustice related
to police brutality and
shootings.
(©2016 Sue Coe. Courtesy Sue Coe.)

SUE COE
Alternative Comics • Cartoonist

Growing up next to a slaughterhouse had a pro-
found impact on Sue Coe's career as an artist. As Coe described it,
"My whole childhood was listening to the pigs scream" (Plotczyk 2016). In
witnessing the horrors of factory farming, Coe decided that her work should
bring to light the atrocities in the world around us. Her stark and sobering

work isn't just limited to farms—Coe has used art to address the horrors of apartheid, systemic racism, HIV, war, and terrorism.

Born in 1951 in England, Coe moved to the United States in 1972. Her highly political work has been featured in *The New York Times*, *The Nation*, *Entertainment Weekly*, *The Progressive*, *The New Yorker*, *Rolling Stone*, *Artforum*, and several other publications. In 1983, Françoise Mouly and Art Spiegelman's RAW Books published Coe's first book, an examination of the cruelties of apartheid called *How to Commit Suicide in South Africa*. In 1986, Raw released Coe's second book, *X*, which was meant to be "a visual complement to the *Autobiography of Malcolm X*" (Heller 1996).

Coe uses her artwork to address social issues, often juxtaposing victims and perpetrators in evocative and impactful ways, conveying dreadful events such that they cannot be ignored by the viewer. Because Coe's work is so powerful and unabashedly political, it has occasionally run afoul of censors. *Woman Walks into Bar—Is Raped by Four Men on the Pool Table—While 20 Watch* (sometimes referred to as "The Rape of Rosa Velez"), an oversized painting that graphically depicts the gang rape of a woman, has been attacked on multiple occasions. Coe submitted an early version of the piece—which is based on a true story—for a magazine assignment, but the publication cropped the image to obscure the more violent aspects, removing much of the artwork's impact. In 1984, British authorities temporarily shut down a portion of an exhibition at Ferens Gallery in the U.K. because a city councilor thought the painting was "too

disturbing." The organizer of the exhibit hired lawyers who were able to get the work reinstated after pointing out that the censorship violated the contract the city had signed and that the piece was not in violation of British indecency and obscenity laws (Lydiate 1984).

Coe uses various media, including paint, collage, drawing, and block prints, but she considers herself more a journalist than an artist. Coe does extensive research for each of her projects. For *Dead Meat* (1996), which collects many of her pieces about factory farms and slaughterhouses, Coe visited stockyards, meatpacking plants, dairies, and chicken farms to sketch the atrocities she saw there. She did the same for *Sheep of Fools* (2005) and *Cruel* (2012).

Coe remains adamant that artwork should be used to address the cruelty of the world around us. Her art is graphic, angry, and hard to ignore, as Steven Heller wrote in a 1996 profile of Coe:

> Coe has lost none of her anger, but she has learned how to control it. It is the anger that has given her the strength to experience atrocity and horror, and emerge ennobled. It is the anger, as well as the compassion and commitment, that allows her to bear witness when most of us are too timid even to get involved.

FURTHER READING

Dead Meat by Sue Coe (Four Walls Eight Windows, 1996)

Cruel: Bearing Witness to Animal Exploitation by Sue Coe (OR Books, 2012)

Sue Coe: The Ghosts of Our Meat by Phillip J. Earenfight and Stephen F. Eisenman (The Trout Gallery/Dickinson College, 2014)

The first appearance of LGBTQ characters D'mer and the Avatar from *A Distant Soil* Volume 1.
(© Colleen Doran. Courtesy Colleen Doran.)

COLLEEN DORAN

Alternative Comics • Cartoonist

An exceptionally precocious artist, Collen Doran won a Disney art contest in the late 1960s at the age of **five.** At that time she had every intention of eventually becoming an animator, but she also felt pulled to comics. At 12 years old, a lengthy bout with pneumonia unexpectedly cemented her career track in two ways: a friend of her father's gifted her a huge box of comics to read while bedridden, and she had lots of time to write and draw her own creations. It was at that early juncture that she began work on her long-running independent series *A Distant Soil*, which has since become a touchstone in self-published comics.

By the time she went to college, Doran was already working full time as an artist, and *A Distant Soil* was being published by WaRP Graphics. After a dispute over alterations to the work and copyright ownership, however, Doran left WaRP and started the series over again at Starblaze Graphics, an imprint of the Donning Company.

After Donning in turn went out of business, Doran worked for a time on major properties, including *Amazing Spider-Man*, *Wonder Woman*, *The Sandman*, and *Legion of Superheroes*. A Marvel adventure comic she illustrated in 1986, *Swords of the Swashbucklers* #9, was one of the books seized in the police raid of Friendly Frank's comic shop, which led to the establishment of CBLDF. The issue was reportedly targeted due to lesbian themes, but ultimately was dropped from the case before store manager Michael Correa was prosecuted for the display of obscene materials.

Having been burned in her previous attempts to find a publisher for *A Distant Soil*, in 1991 Doran decided to take on the job herself. Through her own company, Aria Press, she re-released the issues that had been published by now-defunct Donning, and then continued the story with new material. In 1995 the series was picked up by Image Comics, which still publishes it to this day.

Heavily influenced by manga, *A Distant Soil* was among the first U.S. comics to feature openly LGBTQ characters. In a 1995 interview in *Comics Buyer's Guide*, Doran said she saw no reason not to include characters of all orientations:

> I thought I was pretty obvious. Rieken and D'mer are lovers and bisexual... I do plan to explore gay rights concerns at greater length in the future. Gay rights are human rights, and I don't care if people think I'm a lesbian. Just shows how homophobic they are. Like straight people can't support gay rights! That's like saying men can't be feminists! Really stupid.

Doran is credited as a pioneer in self-publishing and continues to advocate tirelessly for creators' rights. Her recent portfolio is as diverse as ever. In 2012 she illustrated the multi-generational Irish American family saga *Gone to Amerikay*, written by Derek McCulloch. Recently, she worked on Stan Lee's memoir *Amazing Fantastic Incredible* and a graphic novel adaptation of Neil Gaiman's short story "Troll Bridge." In between, she has drawn covers for *The Walking Dead*, *Squirrel Girl*, and *S.H.I.E.L.D.*, among many others.

FURTHER READING

A Distant Soil (multiple volumes) by Colleen Doran (Image Comics)

The Sandman (multiple volumes and editions) by Neil Gaiman and various artists (DC Comics)

Gone to Amerikay by Derek McCulloch and Colleen Doran (Vertigo, 2012)

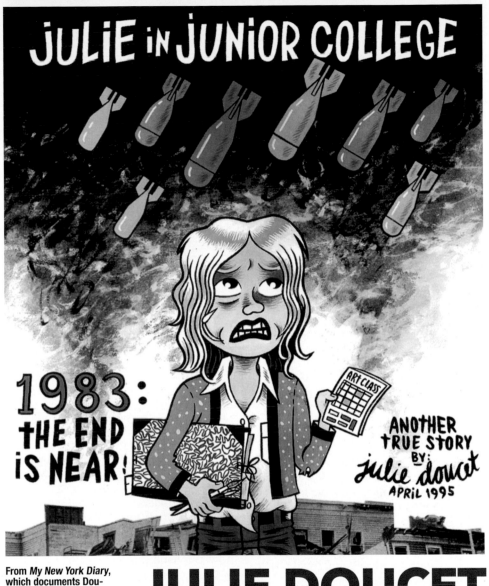

JULIE DOUCET

Alternative Comics • Cartoonist

From *My New York Diary*,
which documents Dou-
cet's time in the city.

(©2013 Julie Doucet. Courtesy Drawn &
Quarterly.)

Frank, funny, and sometimes shocking, Julie
Doucet grew up in Montreal. While there, she attended an all-girls
Catholic high school and later obtained a degree in printing arts from Uni-
versité du Québec à Montréal.

In the late 1980s she began working with experimental comics, including
her fanzine *Dirty Plotte*, which was originally self-published but was picked

up by Drawn & Quarterly in 1991. In fact, it was the first standalone comic issued by the now legendary independent comics publisher. That series, says D+Q, "changed the landscape of alternative cartooning, offering a frank, funny, and sometimes shocking melange of dreams, diaries, and stories." In a review of the first three issues of *Dirty Plotte*, *Entertainment Weekly* wrote "*Dirty Plotte...* is the kind of comic book that often winds up banned" (De Haven 1991). Fortunately, CBLDF hasn't had to defend the book, which *EW* also called "unsettling, but funny too." Anne Elizabeth Moore, founding editor of the *Best American Comics* series, summed up *Dirty Plotte* for Bitch Media:

> These were the things that *Dirty Plotte* was about: the isolation of being a driven female creative; the jealousy in personal relationships that come out of that; the ever-present push from the outside to be maternal and nurturing, but the absolute interior knowledge that that is not your way; and the incredibly shifting sense of gender that a strong, smart woman must feel in order to move about in the world. (2009)

The 1990s were dynamic years for Doucet, as she moved from Montreal to New York to Seattle to Berlin and finally back to Montreal in 1998. Her time in New York, she says dryly on her website, "didn't go too well," and was chronicled in *My New York Diary* in 1999. During those years D+Q also published two collections of her strips, which had originally appeared in alt-weeklies and other periodicals. After returning to her hometown, she ended *Dirty Plotte* and started a new strip about life in Montreal called *The Madame Paul Affair*, which was published in collected form in 2000.

After that, Doucet declared that she was done with the comics format—too much work for not enough money, she says—and has since thrown herself into an astounding variety of other artforms, including silkscreen printmaking, collage poetry, animation, and papier-mâché sculpture, all tinged with the same wry humor and bustling energy that fans know from her earlier work.

Despite Doucet's contention that she was leaving comics, reviewers noted a certain sequentiality that persisted in subsequent works, such as the collection of art prints *Long Time Relationship*, and suggested that she had in fact redefined what comics could be rather than leaving them. In a 2014 profile for *Artforum International*, Hillary Chute outlined Doucet's enduring influence:

> Doucet is central to our understanding of comics as a particularly vibrant platform for telling and showing women's stories. Her work in the 1990s ushered in an era of comics as a feminist art form—a shift we can note throughout the past twenty years, marked by the success of Marjane Satrapi's *Persepolis* (2000) and Alison Bechdel's *Fun Home: A Family Tragicomic* (2006).

Doucet still lives in Montreal, where she now publishes her own work through her press Le Pantalitaire and is deeply involved in the arts community.

FURTHER READING

My New York Diary by Julie Doucet (Drawn & Quarterly, 2013)

My Most Secret Desire by Julie Doucet (Drawn & Quarterly, 2006)

Elle-Humour by Julie Doucet (Picture Box, 2006)

From *Lost Girls*,
written by Alan Moore
and illustrated by
Melinda Gebbie.

MELINDA GEBBIE

Underground Comix / Alternative Comics • Cartoonist

Melinda Gebbie began her career as a fine artist but found a home among the underground comix creators in her birthplace of San Francisco, California.

Her first comics work was published in the seminal all-women underground comix anthology *Wimmen's Comix,* and she published her first solo work in 1977 with the release of *Fresca Zizis.* The brightly colored, dreamy, and explicit images that graced the 36 pages of *Fresca Zizis* would eventually catch the eye of U.K. censors when Knockabout Comics imported 400 copies of the book in 1985. The books were seized by U.K. customs for pornographic images, and despite Gebbie's eloquent defense of the book during the subsequent obscenity trial, British authorities ruled that the copies should be confiscated and burned. Possession of the comic remains a crime in the U.K. today.

A brush with UK censors didn't stop Gebbie from continuing her groundbreaking work. She is best known to many for her labor of love, *Lost Girls*. Alongside writer Alan Moore, Gebbie sought to create a piece of literate erotica that focused on three central characters: Dorothy Gale (*The Wizard of Oz*), Wendy Darling (*Peter Pan*), and Alice Fairchild (*Alice in Wonderland*). Gebbie and Moore set their story against tumultuous events contemporary with the adult versions of the characters, including the release of Igor Stravinsky's *The Rite of Spring*, the assassination of Archduke Franz Ferdinand, and the start of World War I. Gebbie's artwork is lush and sensuous, and Gebbie has attributed the 16 years she spent on the three-volume series with expanding her own artistic sensibility and skill.

Many expected that *Lost Girls* would meet with immediate controversy upon its release, but the book has actually met with little resistance in the United States. While some retailers refuse to carry the book, and it has met resistance in foreign markets (most notably, the U.K. and New Zealand), Gebbie's sensitive, colorful, and painterly artwork can be credited in no small part for keeping the work from being labeled obscene.

Gebbie's work and subject matter may not appeal to everyone, but Gebbie has always sought to depict female sexuality in a positive manner, sometimes to the derision and even overt hostility of male colleagues. During a 2013 talk at the Edinburgh Book Festival, she described some of her opponents: "They were some of the most backward guys in terms of their fears and belief systems, and their sexism. They were classical-

Melinda Gebbie's cover for *Wimmen's Comix #7*
(Released December 1976. Courtesy Fantagraphics)

ly untrained in the consciousness of appreciating women" (Sneddon 2013). She works to overcome this attitude with her art, and she takes an equally strong stance against censorship, even for material that she doesn't like, telling Edinburgh attendees, "I don't think the imagination should ever be policed because it's in the imagination landscape that we work out some of these crucial issues before we have to act them out on the world stage" (Sneddon 2013).

FURTHER READING

The Complete Wimmen's Comix edited by Trina Robbins (Fantagraphics, 2016)

Lost Girls by Alan Moore and Melinda Gebbie (Top Shelf Productions, 2009)

From Gloeckner's examination of teenage female sexuality, *The Diary of a Teenage Girl.*

(Revised edition, p. 213. ©2015 Phoebe Gloeckner. Courtesy North Atlantic Books.)

PHOEBE GLOECKNER

Underground Comix / Alternative Comics • Cartoonist

Phoebe Gloeckner grew up in the **San Francisco Bay Area, which many know as the birthplace of underground comix.** As a child, Gloeckner met several of the artists behind the irreverent—and frequently banned—underground comix. A devoted fan of Aline Kominsky-Crumb and Diane Noomin's *Twisted Sisters* and acquainted with several members of the underground scene, Gloeckner would share her work with some of the biggest names in comix. "Even then I thought she was way better than many cartoonists who were already in print," recalls Noomin (Joiner 2003).

Gloeckner would go on to publish stories in *Wimmen's Comix*, *Weirdo*, and *Young Lust*. Despite her early success as a teenager, Gloeckner didn't immediately set out to be a comic book artist. Instead, she studied medical illustration, eventually earning a Master's from the University of Texas and establishing herself as an artist of human anatomy.

Gloeckner's comics work continued to be sporadic until 1998, when she released her first stand-alone graphic collection, *A Child's Life and Other Stories*. Through a series of interconnected strips, *A Child's Life* conveys the loss of innocence that comes with emotional and physical abuse during childhood. In 2002, Gloeckner released *The Diary of a Teenage Girl*, which combines prose and illustration to continue the story of some of the characters from *A Child's Life*. In *The Diary of a Teenage Girl*, Gloeckner explores the repercussions of secret sexual relationship between a 15-year-old girl and her mother's 35-year-old boyfriend.

While Gloeckner is reticent to describe just how closely the books correlate to her own life, many consider them semi-autobiographical. The artwork in both books is dynamic and heavily influenced by the undergrounds, and Gloeckner incorporates medical illustrations to evocative and sometimes shocking effect.

Gloeckner's work includes themes of coming of age and sexual awaking and contains references to sex, drugs, and STIs, so it is intended for mature audiences. But in 2004, *A Child's Life* was removed from public library shelves in Stockton, California, after an 11-year-old boy checked out the book. Upon discovering graphic content in the book, the boy's mother reproduced images from it and leafleted the community with them in protest of what she considered unacceptable material in the public library. Library director Nicky Stanke believed the book worthy of inclusion in the library's collection, but then-mayor Gary Podesto disagreed, calling the book "a how-to book for pedophiles" (Kinsella 2004) and demanding that the city council exert more control over the library's collection. In response, CBLDF joined the National Coalition Against Censorship and the American Library Association to create guidelines for librarians about handling graphic novels intended for adult audiences.

In 2015 an acclaimed motion picture adaptation of *The Diary of a Teenage Girl* was released. The book also faced a confidential challenge for its mature themes in an undisclosed location, but CBLDF's defense of the book helped ensure that it remained on the shelves.

FURTHER READING

The Diary of a Teenage Girl, Revised Edition: An Account in Words and Pictures by Phoebe Gloeckner (North Atlantic Books, 2015)

A Child's Life and Other Stories by Phoebe Gloeckner (Frog Books, 2000)

The Complete Wimmen's Comix edited by Trina Robbins (Fantagraphics, 2016)

Panels from *Good Girls* #1, exhibiting Lay's signature surrealistic humor.

(Published by Fantagraphics, April 1987. Courtesy Carol Lay.)

CAROL LAY
Alternative Comics • Cartoonist

From the 1970s to today, Carol Lay has successfully bridged the gaps among underground, independent, and mainstream comics. From surreal pastiche of classic genre books to new frontiers in graphic journalism and memoir, she is constantly innovating to drive her art and the industry forward.

The first issue of *Good Girls*.
(Published by Fantagraphics, April 1987. Courtesy Carol Lay.)

Lay grew up in Orange County, California, during the 1950s, a time and place in which she says "the normality was mind-numbing." She was able to step outside the mundane through TV shows like *The Twilight Zone* and *Alfred Hitchcock Presents*, but didn't fully escape it until she attended UCLA, where she "discovered Frank Zappa and *Zap Comix* in the first week." Lay had a wide variety of interests but majored in fine arts, although she was already frustrated with the field before she finished her degree.

After college Lay was drawn to the practical discipline of commercial art. She worked in ad design for a few years until she hit upon the idea of creating comics, which she says suited her "skills and interests in drawing, storytelling, logic, and complex puzzle solving."

Lay got her start in the industry through lettering, then took on various jobs at comics publishers, including DC, Marvel, Hanna-Barbera, and Western Publishing. Meanwhile, she continued in commercial art and illustration for Mattel and drew storyboards for both live-action and animated films. Lay expressed her more surreal sensibilities through her own independent comic *Good Girls*, a parody of romance comics that features an heiress who was adopted by an African tribe as an infant and received drastic facial modifications.

Throughout the 1990s and 2000s, Lay found her niche with her strip *WayLay*. The strip featured stand-alone slice-of-life stories, economically packed into a page or half-page of panels and featuring characters who often wore sheepish sideways grins. The strip appeared for 18 years in various periodicals and on Salon.com. In 2008 she published a pragmatic and honest graphic memoir about weight loss called *The Big Skinny: How I Changed My Fattitude*. In January 2015, Lay launched a new online strip, *Lay Lines*, which bears the hallmarks of her surrealistic humor and mixes new content with newly-colored versions of her older work. She also recently crowdfunded *Murderville: A Farewell to Armories*, in which "a semi-retired mobster and his family face down a sexy villain on a quaint Maine island."

FURTHER READING

Goodnight, Irene: The Collected Stories of Irene Van de Kamp by Carol Lay (Last Gasp, 2007)

The Big Skinny: How I Changed My Fattitude by Carol Lay (Villard, 2008)

**Wendy Pini's cover art-
work for the first volume
of _The Complete Elfquest._**

WENDY PINI
Independent Comics • Cartoonist

Wendy Pini discovered comic books as a teenager in the 1960s, devouring them alongside science fiction and fantasy novels. Pini was undeterred by the fact that, as a woman, she wasn't necessarily the target market for the comics and books she read. She soon began drawing her own illustrations, drawing inspiration from the fantasy and science fiction she read (she also drew the ire of at least

one high school art teacher who tried to discourage Pini's fascination with the fantastic). She also embraced fandom, becoming a fixture at fantasy and sci-fi conventions, where she was well-known for intricate cosplay.

During the early 1970s, the largely self-taught Pini illustrated covers for DC and Marvel as well as science fiction and fantasy magazines such as *Galaxy*, *Galileo*, and *Worlds of If*. In 1978, Pini, alongside her husband Richard, launched what has become one of the longest-running independent comics series: *Elfquest*.

During a CBLDF panel at Comic-Con 2016, Pini described the start of *Elfquest* and the decision to publish independently:

> We finally landed on the idea of doing a comic because it was a way of blending the things that we could do: the writing and the drawing together. So, we made up some samples and took it around—Marvel, DC, you know, anybody. And they all found it... well, I guess the adjective was "peculiar."

> They found it to be too peculiar for their interests at the time. So, one thing and another happened, and Richard [Pini], bless him, decided to educate himself in the art of publishing, and we thought "well, let's just bring it out ourselves!"

In *Elfquest*, Pini created a diverse cast of characters and frequently addressed contemporary social issues through her stories and illustrations. Pini's artwork in *Elfquest* is inspired in part by Japanese manga and looked nothing like the work that dominated comics at the time the series launched. Her characters were more androgynous and gender fluid, and the artwork was notably feminine and sensual. When *Elfquest* debuted in *Fantasy Quarterly* #1, it became an in-stant hit, especially among female comics fans. Now in circulation for nearly 40 years, the series has a loyal and broad fanbase and is considered by many a touchstone of independent comics.

At Comic-Con 2016, Pini also described some of the specific appeal of the series:

> *Elfquest* has always been very subversive because on the surface, when you look at it—especially if you're a super hero fan and don't really know that much about fantasy—you're looking at what appears to be cute little elves, but underneath it all... *Elfquest* has always been about the condition of life, and it's always been about relationships.

Elfquest often depicts issues and events that aren't commonly subjects of the comics medium. An issue in the *Elfquest: New Blood* series, published in the early 1990s, included panels that focused on childbirth. The imagery included partial nudity, but the event was tastefully illustrated and conveyed as life-affirming. Unfortunately, someone in West Virginia didn't agree. In 1999, a social worker gave a neighborhood boy a copy of the comic, and the boy's grandfather contacted authorities after a verbal altercation. Dragged from his bed in the middle of the night and arrested for distributing obscene materials to a minor, the social worker contacted CBLDF for assistance. The comic came nowhere near failing the Miller test for obscenity, so CBLDF legal counsel Burton Joseph was able to get the charges dismissed in preliminary hearings.

FURTHER READING

The Complete Elfquest (multiple volumes) by Wendy and Richard Pini (Dark Horse Comics)

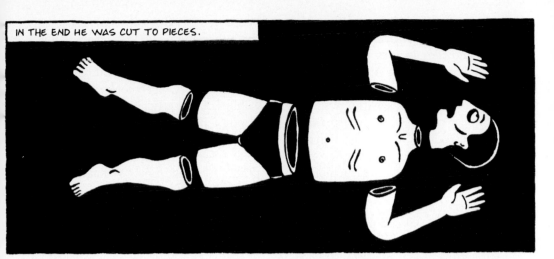

IN THE END HE WAS CUT TO PIECES.

**Excerpt from p. 52
of Marjane Satrapi's
Persepolis, depicting
the dismemberment of
political prisoners.**
(©2003 Marjane Satrapi. Published by Pantheon, a division of Random House LLC.)

MARJANE SATRAPI
Alternative Comics • Cartoonist

In the early 2000s Marjane Satrapi's *Persepolis* **set a new standard for graphic novel memoirs of childhood amidst turmoil.** Taking an inside look at the brutality and absurdity that overtook her native Iran in the 1980s, Satrapi's book met with resounding success among casual readers as well as educators and librarians, who embraced its capacity for increasing cultural understanding. Nevertheless, the book has also been challenged numerous times over the years by those who do not appreciate its unflinching account of reality.

Anyone who's read *Persepolis* is already familiar with the key events of Satrapi's early life. Growing up in Tehran during the turmoil surrounding the Islamic Revolution, Satrapi experienced abrupt changes that curtailed the secular lifestyle she and her intellectual parents had enjoyed prior to 1979. Always rebellious and bluntly inquisitive, she began to act out even more in school and in public after her favorite uncle was killed in prison. For her own safety, Satrapi's parents sent her alone to attend high school in Austria when she was 14, in 1984. She returned to Iran at 18 and obtained a Master's degree in visual communication from Tehran's School of Fine Arts, but found the prospect of remaining in the country under the repressive regime untenable. In 1994 she moved to Strasbourg, France, where she continued to study art, and on to Paris three years later.

Satrapi often regaled her friends in France with stories of her surreal childhood, and they in turn introduced her to comics, including Art Spiegelman's *Maus*. She had been dabbling in children's picture books without success, but Spiegelman's work proved that illustrated books could engage with more serious subjects. Satrapi decided to try her hand at a graphic novel memoir, and produced *Persepolis* in four volumes between 2000 and 2003. They met with immediate critical and popular acclaim in France and were published in two volumes for the U.S. market in 2003 and 2004. In 2007 Satrapi co-wrote and directed the animated movie based on the comics. The film tied for the Jury Prize at the Cannes Film Festival, won two French Césars, and was nominated for an Oscar and a Golden Globe.

While it's hardly surprising that both the books and movie have been banned in Iran, *Persepolis* has also seen more than its fair share of trouble in U.S. schools. Most spectacularly, Chicago Public Schools officials made a confused attempt in March 2013 to remove the book from all classrooms due to "graphic language and content that is inappropriate for children" (Williams 2015). They allowed it to remain in AP classes for grades 11 and 12, but now require grade 8–10 teachers to undergo extra training before they can use the book in class. The book remains banned in grade 7 classrooms. In 2014 there were two more school challenges to *Persepolis* in quick succession: one in the Three Rivers School District in Oregon, and another in Illinois in the Ball-Chatham district. The challenges failed in both locations, and the book was restored without restriction.

In a rare higher education challenge, *Persepolis* was one of four graphic novels that a 20-year-old college student and her parents wanted "eradicated from the system" at Crafton Hills College in Yucaipa, California. Crafton Hills administrators supported the instructor, but suggested the graphic novel course will include a disclaimer "so students have a better understanding of the course content." CBLDF led the National Coalition Against Censorship in protest of this attack on academic freedom, and the district backed away from the proposed disclaimer plan.

Artwork from page 51 of *Persepolis*, one of the pages contested in the Chicago Public School system's attempted ban.

(©2003 Marjane Satrapi. Published by Pantheon, a division of Random House LLC.)

FURTHER READING

The Complete Persepolis by Marjane Satrapi (Pantheon, 2007)

Ariel Schrag explores her own coming out in her *High School Comic Chronicles* series.

(From *Likewise*, p. 152, Touchstone, 2009. Courtesy Ariel Schrag.)

ARIEL SCHRAG
Alternative Comics • Cartoonist

When it comes to autobiographical comics, few creators are as precocious as Ariel Schrag. Before Schrag had even finished high school, renowned independent publisher Slave Labor Graphics had begun releasing her comics, which explored the mundane aspects of high school existence with aplomb. But they delved into deeper territory than expected for a creator so young: Schrag's coming out.

Openly LGBTQ, Schrag's ambitious and confessional work has been widely praised, drawing comparisons to notables such as Alison Bechdel, Judy Blume, and R. Crumb. Her work honestly confronts coming of age, sexual awakening, and sexual identity, often with sharp and mesmerizing humor. It began with her *High School Comic Chronicles* series: *Awkward and Definition* (1997), *Potential* (1999), and *Likewise* (2000). Yet, Schrag hasn't limited herself to graphic novels. She's written for television—most notably for the Showtime series *The L Word*—provided articles and illustrations for periodicals around the country, been the featured subject of a documentary, and edited comics anthologies.

It was Schrag's role as an editor that brought her to the attention of censors: In late 2011, CBLDF joined the ALA Office for Intellectual Freedom in writing a letter to the superintendent of the Dixfield, Maine, school system in order to prevent the removal of the anthology *Stuck in the Middle: Seventeen Comics from an Unpleasant Age* from library shelves. Schrag edited *Stuck in the Middle*, and it includes contributions from acclaimed graphic novelists Daniel Clowes, Dash Shaw, Gabrielle Bell, Lauren Weinstein, and more.

The school had received a complaint objecting to language, sexual content, and drug references in the book. In the letter to Dixfield, CBLDF shared Schrag's defense of the book that resulted from a 2009 ban in Sioux Falls, South Dakota:

> In terms of foul language, sexual content, and teen smoking in this book, all the authors strove to present the teens and pre-teens in a realistic light. We may not like all of the decisions teenagers make, but if we sanitize their speech and behavior in our stories, our characters won't be authentic. Real teens and pre-teens sometimes use these words and say and do these things. A book like this can present a good opportunity for dialogue between children and parents. Banning the book isn't going to change children's behavior or somehow save them from the hard truths of teenage life—I find it very hard to believe that a child would hear a swear word for the very first time in the book,

or that he or she would be made aware that teenagers sometimes have sexual relationships or smoke cigarettes. The only thing that can make an impact in the way children act is communication, and this book provides a platform for that. (Schrag 2013)

Ultimately, the school board voted to leave the book on library shelves with the caveat that students must have parental permission to check it out.

Schrag hasn't let the spectre of censorship keep her from publishing groundbreaking examinations of marginalized LGBTQ characters. In 2014, she released *Adam*, which explores the queer community of New York City through the eyes of a straight 17-year-old boy who pretends to be a trans man. Schrag tells Svetlana Kitto about the decision to center her story on the deceit of a privileged cisgendered male:

> I liked the idea of writing a book about this world but filtering it through the ideas of somebody aligned with the mainstream. It could give me a chance to address all the judgments and confusion that people have head-on, without having to be didactic. And it could also open people's minds in a way that you can't when you enter a subculture within a subculture because you still see it as an Other. I thought having the mainstream enter that Other would be a good way to write about it. (2014)

FURTHER READING

Adam by Ariel Schrag (Mariner Books, 2015)

Awkward and Definition by Ariel Schrag (Touchstone, 2008)

Potential by Ariel Schrag (Touchstone, 2008)

Likewise by Ariel Schrag (Touchstone, 2009)

**Posy Simmonds' cover
art for *Tamara Drewe*.**
(Published by Jonathan Cape, 2009.
©2007 Posy Simmonds.)

POSY
SIMMONDS
Alternative Comics • Cartoonist

Rosemary Simmonds, nicknamed Posy, was born in 1945 and grew up on her family's dairy farm in Berkshire, England. The middle of five children in a well-off family, she

stoked her artistic talent early by browsing back issues of the touchstone satirical magazine *Punch*. She later recalled in an interview in *The Guardian*, "that if I drew a fairy very well people would say it was good. But if I then made her smoke a cigarette, people would laugh" (Wroe 2010).

After attaining high marks at boarding school, Simmonds studied art at the Sorbonne in Paris and the Central School of Art and Design in London. After obtaining her degree, she made a meager living off of freelance illustration, later telling *The Guardian*'s Nicholas Wroe that her best-paying gigs were for *Reader's Digest*, which gave artists "wonderful instructions: 'No smoking, no drinking, no sex, no big noses.'" In 1969 she debuted a daily comic strip called *Bear* in the tabloid paper *The Sun*, and subsequently worked her way into more highbrow publications, such as *Cosmopolitan*, *Harper's*, and *The Guardian* itself, which would become her home base over the following decades.

From 1977 to 1987, *The Guardian* ran Simmonds' strip *Posy*, which skewered the British bourgeoisie that was her own milieu. Reviewer Michael Barber predicted that "in a hundred years' time, she will be required reading for social historians" because of her talent for loading characters down with subtle status symbols and convincingly portraying their way of speaking. Simmonds also continued freelance illustrations for periodicals and published several offbeat and inventive children's picture books, such as *Fred*, about two siblings who discover that their recently deceased cat led a secret life as a feline rock star.

In 1999 Simmonds broke new ground with *Gemma Bovery*, a graphic novel update of and homage to Flaubert's *Madame Bovary*. Much like the original Emma Bovary, Simmonds' bored adulteress eventually meets a tragic end— but Gemma Bovery is a modern-day middle-class Englishwoman living in France, and reviewer David Hughes proclaimed that the book encapsulates

"all that ever needs to be said about the English trying to settle in France, the unsettling nature of the French, the nature of culture clash, lurk[ing] with sly hilarity."

Gemma Bovery was initially serialized in *The Guardian* before it was released in book form, a pattern Simmonds repeated in 2007 with her next graphic novel, *Tamara Drewe*. This was also inspired by a classic novel, Thomas Hardy's *Far From the Madding Crowd*, but that parentage is less obvious than in *Gemma Bovery*. A review in *The New Yorker* compared the book's "lushly realistic drawings and complex female characters" to those of Alison Bechdel, but added that Simmonds' "learned references and her ear for a variegated British vernacular make her unique" (Walker 2008). Both *Tamara Drewe* and *Gemma Bovery* have been adapted into films.

In recent years Simmonds has continued to do freelance illustration and cartoons for various periodicals, including *The Guardian*, and is now lauded as one of the bright lights of British cartooning. In 2012 her work was featured in a large exhibition at the Belgian Comics Centre in Brussels, and in 2015 she was invited to present a career retrospective at the Queen's Gallery in the Buckingham Palace complex.

FURTHER READING

Tamara Drewe by Posy Simmonds (Jonathan Cape, 2009)

Gemma Bovery by Posy Simmonds (Pantheon, 2005)

Fred by Posy Simmonds (Andersen Press, 2014)

This One Summer is the first graphic novel to receive the Caldecott honor.

(*This One Summer*, pp. 84–85. ©2014 Jillian Tamaki and Mariko Tamaki. Courtesy First Second.)

JILLIAN & MARIKO TAMAKI

Alternative Comics • Cartoonist & Writer

Canadian cousins Jillian and Mariko Tamaki both came to graphic novels somewhat unconventionally. Jillian started out (and continues) as a freelance illustrator for books and periodicals, including *The New York Times*, *Esquire*, and *The New Yorker*, while Mariko cut her teeth in the performance art and comedy scenes of Montreal and Toronto. Growing up on opposite sides of the country—Jillian in Calgary and Mariko in Toronto—they both evinced a rebellious streak as teens. Mariko in particular experienced alienation from her peers as "a weird, freaky, gothy kid" (*Sequential Tart*) at an elite private boarding school, while Jillian attended public school and says she and her friends were "disaffected, kinda gothy—they called us 'the dirties' in high school" (Randle 2011).

Both cousins were well-established in their creative careers before they struck upon the idea of collaborating. Mariko was offered the chance to publish some of her stage monologues in comics form as part of a zine series that Jillian says aimed "to pair people who had never written a comic and people who had never drawn a comic" (Randle 2011). Mariko naturally thought of her illustrator cousin, and together they produced a 24-page comic which would later become the 2008 graphic novel *Skim*. Loosely inspired by Mariko's boarding school experience, it became the first graphic novel nominated for Canada's prestigious Governor General's Award—but only in the text category. This prompted several comics creators to issue an open letter arguing that neither the text nor the illustrations are meant to stand alone, and both Tamakis should have been nominated.

Although the selective nomination put both Jillian and Mariko in an awkward public situation, it apparently didn't harm their collaborative relationship. In 2014, they released *This One Summer*, a coming-of-age story of adolescent friends Rose and Windy. This time, the book was nominated for Governor General's Awards for both text and illustration and won in the latter category. In an interview about the win, Jillian addressed how the award disregards the dual nature of comics:

I think we are both creators of the book. You can't read a comic without either component, it won't make sense. It's something I will always be addressing when talking about the award. But I am completely flattered by the honour and will be sharing the prize with my cousin. (Volmers 2014)

This One Summer also broke another barrier in the U.S., where it became the first graphic novel to make the shortlist for the American Library Association's Caldecott Medal. It was also shortlisted for ALA's Printz Award for young adult literature, which previously went to Gene Luen Yang's *American Born Chinese* in 2007.

The Caldecott Honor led to some rather unexpected backlash. A few people, believing the book was aimed at younger readers because it is a Caldecott Honor Book, have been shocked to find that the award winning graphic novel is intended for audiences age 12 and up. Instead of acknowledging their responsibility for knowing the content of a book before purchasing it, some of these people have instead attacked the book, calling for its removal.

Since the Caldecott honor was announced, CBLDF has been confidentially involved in monitoring and preventing challenges to *This One Summer* in various communities. It was subjected to a biased media attack in Seminole County, Florida. Most notably, the book was banned in the K–12 library in the small community of Henning, Minnesota. After CBLDF led a coalition of freedom-to-read advocates in protest of the ban, the school system restored the book but the school board decided that even students in grades 10–12 must have signed parental permission to read it.

FURTHER READING

This One Summer by Jillian and Mariko Tamaki (First Second, 2014)

Skim by Mariko and Jillian Tamaki (Groundwood Books, 2008)

Overtly feminist, *Bitch Planet* is a send-up of the women in prison exploitation film.

(*Bitch Planet* © Milkfed Criminal Masterminds, Inc. Artwork by Valentine De Landro. Courtesy Image Comics.)

KELLY SUE DECONNICK

Modern Age • Writer

Dubbed the "Future of Women in Comics" by *Vanity Fair* (Parker 2015), Kelly Sue DeConnick is changing an industry that has historically left out women.** Because of DeConnick and the generation of female comics creators of which she is part, women are flocking to comic books in unheard of numbers.

In 2012, DeConnick would take on a title that marked a sea change in contemporary mainstream comics: *Captain Marvel*. In this incarnation, Carol Danvers would wear the mantle of Captain Marvel. It wouldn't be the first time a woman—or even Carol Danvers—bore the name, but the series would fundamentally alter the way women were represented in comics. As DeConnick tells Sonia Saraiya at *Salon*:

I wanted to write about female friendships. That's one thing I can say I consciously did, was I wanted to write about female friendships in a way that I don't get to see enough of in popular culture. (2015)

DeConnick would conclude her groundbreaking run in 2015 with three dozen issues. Despite a devout fan following and accolades—*Comics Alliance* dubbed Carol Danvers "Marvel's biggest female hero" in 2014—DeConnick's run on *Captain Marvel* wasn't without backlash. A small number of people accused DeConnick of inserting "her feminist agenda" (Saraiya 2015) into the series, criticism that DeConnick didn't expect but took to heart. The negative attention would ultimately help inspire DeConnick's hit series with Image Comics, *Bitch Planet*, co-created with Valentine De Landro in 2014. Described by Image as "*A Handmaid's Tale* meets *Inglorious Basterds*," *Bitch Planet* is unapologetically feminist and political. Like *Captain Marvel*, the series has inspired legions of devoted fans, male and female alike. DeConnick and Emma Ríos' feminist western fantasy, *Pretty Deadly*, which Image Comics describes as "beautifully lush" and "unflinchingly savage," also launched in 2014.

In a time when even the mention of the word "feminism" on the internet might launch a virtual nuclear war, DeConnick is fearless about using the term and incorporating feminist ideas into her work. When Saraiya asked DeConnick about why she puts feminism front and center in *Bitch Planet*, DeConnick spoke to several basic truths about comics, from being a format that lends itself to free expression to one that is inherently accommodating to timely ideas:

Well, I mean I think the easy answer is because I can, you know? That's one of the really beautiful things about [comics]: a pretty low threshold of publication. So we can be more responsive than really anything but the web. If you want to, if you are a crazy person, you could go from idea to the stands in about four months. It does not cost hundreds of thousands of dollars to make a comic the way it does to make a television show or a movie. We don't have stockholders to appease. Nobody has to weigh in and tell me who I might offend, you know? So there's enough freedom to hang yourself there, really. Yeah, the easiest answer is because I could, or because we could.

In just a few short years, DeConnick has become one of the driving forces behind the women in comics revolution. DeConnick herself questions what more she has to offer the medium, but colleague (and fellow woman who changed free expression in comics) Gail Simone says, "When I was dreaming of what the future of women in comics could be, I was dreaming of [DeConnick]. I just didn't know it yet" (Parker 2015).

FURTHER READING

Captain Marvel (multiple volumes) by Kelly Sue DeConnick and various artists (Marvel Comics)

Bitch Planet (multiple volumes) by Kelly Sue DeConnick and Valentine De Landro (Image Comics)

Pretty Deadly (multiple volumes) by Kelly Sue DeConnick and Emma Ríos (Image Comics)

The Death of Superman storyline, which Simonson helped write, is one of the bestselling graphic novels of all time.

(Artwork from *Superman* #75, January 1993. Artwork by Dan Jurgens and Brett Breeding. Superman © and ™ DC Comics. Courtesy DC Comics.)

LOUISE SIMONSON

Bronze Age & Modern Age • Writer & Editor

"Girls can have their own clubs, too" (Kotler 2011).

This is how extraordinary comics writer and editor Louise Simonson described the comics industry in a 2011 interview. Never one to be held back or to let socially-assumed boundaries define what she could and could not do in comics, Simonson worked as an editor for Warren Publishing in the 1970s, co-created *Power Pack* and wrote and edited several of Marvel's X-Men books in the 1980s, and played a major role in constructing the seminal *Death and Return of Superman* storyline for DC Comics in the 1990s. According to *Comics Alliance*:

> Louise Simonson has influenced superhero comics to a degree that few women have... [and] while Simonson is no longer writing at the heart of superhero comics, her influence still echoes through DC and Marvel alike. (2016)

Simonson got her start in the industry in 1974, working in the production department and later as an assistant editor for the historically important Warren Publishing—a publisher that bypassed the Comics Code by producing horror stories in magazine form rather than comics. Working at Warren for almost a decade, when Editor Bill Dubay left in 1982, Simonson issued a challenge to publisher James Warren: "Look, I will edit the line for six months on my Assistant Editor salary and I will get it done, I will get it done on schedule." Not only did she become editor of the full line of books, but she was made a vice president. "I was a big fish in a little itty bitty pond," is how the writer describes her experience at Warren (Kotler 2011).

Simonson's tenacity and chutzpah got her noticed by Marvel in the early 80s. Hired by Jim Shooter to edit the line of X-books, Simonson met some opposition due to her gender:

> There were people who were appalled at the idea of me getting anywhere near the real Marvel books: the Fantastic Four, the Avengers, that stuff. I know of one or two people who just didn't think women belonged anywhere near the core titles. (Reisman 2016)

At the time, the X-books were considered second-tier, and Simonson took the resistance in stride. She would make a significant mark, playing a key role in both the *Dark Phoenix* and *Days of Future Past* storylines. She would co-create the popular *Power Pack* series, which debuted in 1984. While working on *X-Factor*, she would also co-create a major villain in the Marvel universe: Apocalypse.

In the 1990s, Simonson began working for DC, where she helped launch *Superman: The Man of Steel* and later played a significant role in the immensely popular *The Death and Return of Superman* storyline.

From Warren, to Marvel, to DC, and a long list of other publishers since, Simonson never let being a woman prevent her from telling the kind of stories she wanted. In fact, she saw that "baggage" as an opportunity to prove that she was better than any male writer or editor in the business. "Honestly, I think the women who make it in superhero comics don't make it because they're as good as the guys," said Simonson. "They make it because they're better than the guys. You have to be. You have to be smarter, you have to work harder" (Kotler 2011).

FURTHER READING

Superman: The Death of Superman by various (DC Comics, 2016)

X-Men: Days of Future Past by various (Marvel Comics, 2014)

Essential X-Factor **(multiple volumes)** by various (Marvel Comics)

Simone's run on *Red Sonja* has given the character agency and complexity.

(Cover detail for *Red Sonja* #8, February 2014. Artwork by Jenny Frison. Red Sonja © and ® Red Sonja LLC. Courtesy Dynamite Entertainment.)

GAIL SIMONE
Modern Age • Writer

In an era during which women have been persecuted and threatened for speaking out about sexism in geekdom, comics writer Gail Simone is an especially bright light for the cause of women in comics. She uses the medium to address, deconstruct, and overcome sexism. She also uses her formidable social media powers for good, fearlessly calling out misogyny in comics and pop culture.

Simone began her crusade for women's free expression in comics by coining the phrase "women in refrigerators" as part of a collective of female comics fans who founded and contributed to a website of the same name in 1999.

The phrase arose in response to a Green Lantern storyline in which Kyle Rayner's girlfriend was murdered by a villain, dismembered, and stuffed into a refrigerator. "I asked the question, 'Is this a trend in comic books where the female characters are only there to forward the male hero's story?'" Simone told Katie Couric in 2015.

While the response to *Women in Refrigerators* was mixed and the website was short lived, it helped start a revolution in the ways female characters were depicted and treated. This is due in no small part to Simone herself, who was offered opportunities to write comics. Simone began her foray into the medium with *The Simpsons* (Bongo Comics), but she soon moved on to superhero comics, writing some of the most popular story arcs for fan-favorite Deadpool.

Simone moved on to DC Comics, helming immensely popular runs on some of DC's flagship properties, including *Wonder Woman*, *Birds of Prey*, and *Batgirl*. Simone wasn't the first female writer to work on *Wonder Woman*, but she was the longest-running, writing 30 issues between 2008 and 2010. She wrote more than 60 issues of *Birds of Prey* before taking on *Batgirl* for DC's New 52.

In Simone's hands, *Batgirl* was one of the most popular series in the New 52, and it saw doubled sales over previous incarnations of the character. In a strange chain of events, Simone was temporarily removed from *Batgirl* in 2012. The events surrounding Simone's release were unclear, with some speculating that it was due to Simone's outspokenness about the lack of women and diversity in the industry, but immediate fan outcry meant she was back on the title

a scant few weeks later. She continued her run through 2014, during which time she introduced the first openly transgender character in mainstream superhero comics, Barbara's roommate Alysia Yeoh.

Recently, Simone took on an icon of pulp cheesecake: Red Sonja. While her work on the character might be perceived as the antithesis of her activism, Simone's run on the title has proven a boon for publisher Dynamite. In an interview with Janelle Asselin, Simone addresses the perception that the book contradicts her feminism:

> I was a fan of the idea of Red Sonja, but the gender politics of the character made her hard to read for me, at times. I said, if I'm coming aboard, I'm not doing this rapey origin. And Dynamite agreed immediately. (2015)

With Simone at the wheel, Red Sonja has transitioned from the chainmail bikinied red-haired pin-up she once was to "the female equivalent of Conan" she was meant to be (Tonik 2015).

Throughout her career, Simone has remained as fiercely independent as her characters, using comics and social media to overcome sexist tropes. She remains a formidable contributor to free expression and an outspoken advocate for women and diversity in comics.

FURTHER READING

Batgirl: The New 52 (multiple volumes) by Gail Simone and various (DC Comics)

Red Sonja (multiple volumes) by Gail Simone and various (Dynamite Entertainment)

Deadpool Classic, Vols. 9 and 10 by Gail Simone and various (Marvel Comics)

The sweeping space opera of *Saga* is centered on one very basic concept: family.

(©Brian K. Vaughan and Fiona Staples. Courtesy Image Comics.)

FIONA STAPLES

Modern Age • Cartoonist

Award-winning Canadian comic artist Fiona Staples has become one of the most recognizable and influential artists in the industry today. Voted top female comic book artist by *Comic Book Resources* in 2015, the co-creator of *Saga* has helped reshape modern comic art and storytelling and opened a new era of independent, diverse, and creator-driven works.

Staples' first foray into published comics was in *About Comics' 24 Hour Comics Day Highlights 2005*. Recognized for her unique style and approach to character building, the artist would then work on *North 40*, *Mystery Society*, and an assortment of titles with DC Comics. Staples also produced cover art for numerous titles and contributed to independent projects like *Beyond: An Anthology of Queer Sci-fi/Fantasy Comics*.

In 2012, with the release of *Saga*—Staples and writer Brian K. Vaughan's epic space opera—the artist soon dominated numerous top creator lists and won dozens of comics awards. "The series' wide appeal rests in no small part on Staples' gorgeously organic and painterly artwork," writes *The Guardian*, "which brings a believable humanity to her fantasy environments and is about as far from stereotypically muscular comic art as can be imagined" (Harrison 2016).

For many, *Saga* has been their entry point into comics. Vaughan credits Staples for that success:

It's gotten a wider audience than we could ever have dreamed of, and it's all down to Fiona. It takes an artist of genius to make inaccessible ideas relatable. She turned a story for no one into a story for just about everyone. (Harrison 2016)

As *The Guardian* also notes, "Staples is one of only a few women artists whose work and name can sell a book on its own" (Harrison 2016).

Staples' emphasis on the human experience, characterization, and world-building made her the perfect candidate to illustrate the 2015 *Archie* reboot with writer Mark Waid. Staples welcomed work on another book, telling the *A.V. Club* that "It's really important to me to stretch different muscles and try to do as many different things as I can so I don't stagnate creatively" (Sava 2015).

Despite the immense success Staples has experienced, her work hasn't been left unscathed by critics. In 2013, *Saga #12* was temporarily made unavailable in the Apple App Store due to misinterpretation of Apple's content policies. The series was listed by the American Library Association as one of the ten most challenged books of 2014 due in part to a challenge at an undisclosed Oregon public library. A patron demanded the removal of *Saga* over sexually explicit content, but the book was ultimately retained.

Staples is a key part of the current push to diversify comics. When asked about the marginalization of women in the comics industry, Staples said:

It's definitely changing, although maybe not as quickly as we'd like. All the corners of the comics world except mainstream superhero books have pretty much agreed that diversity is a positive thing. I think the important thing to do now is create women-friendly books, and that will lead to more female creators in the next generation. (Marcotte 2014)

FURTHER READING

Saga (multiple volumes) by Brian K. Vaughan and Fiona Staples (Image Comics)

Archie, Vol. 1 by Mark Waid and Fiona Staples (Archie Comics, 2016)

North 40 by Aaron Williams and Fiona Staples (Vertigo, 2015)

Jill Thompson's charming art on *Beasts of Burden* draws in readers.

(Artwork from *Beasts of Burden: Animal Rites*, Dark Horse Comics, 2010. Courtesy Dark Horse Comics.)

JILL THOMPSON
Modern Age • Cartoonist

Jill Thompson's career is as diverse and colorful as the work she produces.

From comics to children's books, Thompson has worked on some of the most influential comics ever created, and she has played a role in reviving the kids' comics category.

From DC, Marvel, and Dark Horse to HarperCollins and Sirius Entertainment, the native Chicagoan and graduate of the American Academy of Art has received numerous accolades for her work and become one of the premier voices in several industries. Recognized with multiple Eisner Awards and by the National Cartoonists Society for her work on Neil Gaiman's acclaimed series *The Sandman*, Dark Horse's *Beasts of Burden*, and her own original series *Scary Godmother*, Thompson has dominated the fields of comics and children's books and proved that having a little supernatural fun isn't just for the guys.

Voted number four in *Comic Book Resources* "Top 25 Female Artists of 2015," Brian Cronin writes, "What's absolutely fascinating to me about Jill Thompson is that she is one of the few artists who has become a star artist using two fairly dramatically different art styles." We'd argue she uses more than two styles, from the clean and detailed lines she used for George Perez's *Wonder Woman* and Grant Morrison's *The Invisibles*; to the wistful, fluid, and expressionistic dreams of *Sandman*; to the more stylized, playful, and kid-friendly images of *Scary Godmother*; and on to the painterly fantasies of *Beasts of Burden*. An artistic chameleon, Thompson readily adapts her art style to best accompany a narrative, making her a true master of the comics artform.

One of Thompson's greatest works is her independently produced *Scary Godmother*. After the comics bust of the 1990s, Thompson found herself without work and time to draw. She was also about to become an aunt—all circumstances that led to *Scary God-mother*. "Scary Godmother was one of those perfect storm situations," notes Thompson (Irving 2012). She wanted to make a book "that bridged the gap between children's books and comic books" (Westfield Comics 2001). A hybrid of a kids' picture book and a comic book, *Scary Godmother* recounts the adventures of the Halloween fairy godmother. Most major comics publishers initially rejected it, in large part because they didn't know what to do with a hybrid comic for kids. But Sirius jumped at the opportunity. Soon, Thompson found herself at the forefront of the kids' comics revival. The series spawned two film adaptations from Mainframe Entertainment that ran on Cartoon Network.

Thompson reinvented herself once again in 2009, working on *Beasts of Burden* with writer Evan Dorkin. Her endearing watercolors on the project stand in contrast to the book's dark subject matter, but the artwork provides an emotional impact it might otherwise lack. The series has received several awards, many of them specifically for Thompson's artwork.

Cronin sums it up: "It is always cool when great artists reinvent themselves, but when great artists re-invent themselves and get even GREATER? Well, that's a whole other (awesome) story."

FURTHER READING

Beasts of Burden: Animal Rites by Evan Dorkin and Jill Thompson (Dark Horse Comics, 2010)

Scary Godmother (multiple volumes) by Jill Thompson (Dark Horse Comics)

The Sandman (multiple volumes) by Neil Gaiman and various (DC Comics)

9

8

Yumiko Oshima's *The Star of Cottonland* was the origin of the popular catgirl icon.

(*The Star of Cottonland*, Vol. 1, pp. 8–9. Reprinted by Hakusensha, 1994. Courtesy Frenchy Lunning.)

24 NENGUMI
Mangaka

Born primarily in in Shōwa 24 (1949), these women are known alternately as the Year 24 Group, the Forty-Niners, or the 24 Nengumi. They make up one of the first key groups of female mangaka who are considered to have innovated, created, and revolutionized the category we now celebrate as shōjo manga.

In the 1950s and early 1960s, "the majority of shōjo manga were created by male artists, most of whom also worked in the shōnen genre. The number of professional women artists working in shōjo manga prior to 1960 (most notably, Toshiko Ueda, Masako Watanabe, Hideko Mizuno, and Miyako Maki) could almost be counted on the fingers of one hand. The stories featured primary school girls, and generally fell into one of three categories: humor, horror, or tear-jerker" (Thorn 1996).

The young women of the 24 Nengumi marked the first major point of artistic and narrative injection for women artists into manga and into comics globally. They significantly contributed to the development of a radical family of subgenres in shōjo manga, shifting the category's influences overwhelmingly towards feminist and queer concerns, with stories conceived, created, and drawn primarily by and for girls and women. Among shōjo manga's innovations were emotion-driven panel layouts, in which shifting temporal and fantastical elements introduce *manpu* (the symbology specific to manga) made up of feathers, flowers, puffy clouds, and twinkling stars, all in aid of the narrative process. Works by the 24 Nengumi often examine radically queer issues, including sexuality, gender, and transgender issues. Many of these works are now considered classics of shōjo manga.

Yasuko Aoike

Most of Yasuko Aoike's works are shōjo manga focused on the feminine categories of romance, adventure, and light comedy, but they also contain elements of shōnen-ai or Boys' Love (BL). She is best known for *From Eroica with Love*, which was serialized by Akita Shoten beginning in 1976 and produced several spinoff series. It was licensed in English by CMX (DC Comics' now-defunct manga imprint), which released 15 volumes of the series between 2004 and 2010.

Riyoko Ikeda

Riyoko Ikeda has written and illustrated many shōjo manga, most of which are based on actual historical events, such as the French and Russian Revolutions. Ikeda's work is characterized by foreign settings and themes of androgyny. Her most notable efforts include *The Rose of Versailles* (also known as *Lady Oscar*), which has been adapted for the stage, anime, and as a live-action film.

Toshie Kihara

Toshie Kihara made her professional debut in 1969 with *Kotchi muite Mama!* in *Bessatsu Margaret* and has continued to write mainly historical and BL manga. She is best known for her series *Mari to Shingo*, a romance between two young men in the early Shōwa era that was

From the English translation of Yasuko Aoike's *From Eroica With Love*, which centers on an openly gay main character.
(Volume 2, p. 66. CMX, 2005. Originally published in *Princess*, 1980. Courtesy Frenchy Lunning.)

published in *Hana to Yume* (1979–1984). She received the 1985 Shogakukan Manga Award for shōjo for *Yume no Ishibumi*, which collects short stories with BL themes.

Minori Kimura

Debuting in 1964 at the precocious age of 14 with her story *Picnic* (serialized in *Ribon*), Minori Kimura continued writing stories for magazines such as *COM* and *Ribon Comic* during her school breaks. During the 1960s and early 1970s, she addressed political and historical issues through stories set in Auschwitz, Vietnam, and the slums of Rio de Janeiro. After college, she took a short break from publishing before returning with *Gift* (*Okurimono*), published in 1974 by Shogakukan in *Bessatsu Shōjo Comic*. The story discussed the struggles of elementary school life. Kimura then published her breakout series, *This Side of the Rape Blossom Field* (*Nanohana Hatake no Kochiragawa*), the story of four young college girls living together. She went on to publish in shōjo, seinen, and ladies manga magazines from Akita Shoten and Kodansha.

Yumiko Ōshima

In her Kodansha Manga Award–winning *The Star of Cottonland*, Yumiko Ōshima is credited with popularizing the *kemonomimi* (catgirl), an innocent, child-like character rather than the current sexually aggressive representation. Ōshima approaches profound and disturbing issues in eccentric ways, taking the reader into realms that are unfamiliar and even uncanny. She debuted in 1968 with "Paula's Tears" in the *Weekly Margaret*, and in 2008 received the Tezuka Osamu Cultural Prize Short Story Award for "Gu-gu date Neko de aru."

Nanae Sasaya

Growing up loving Leiji Matsumoto's comics for girls, including *Maria of the Silver Valley* and *Forest of Luna*, and inspired by the work of Shotaro Ishinomori, Nanae Sasaya made her professional debut with *Seagull* in *Ribon*'s January 1970 issue. Her works embrace the uncanny horrors of everyday life, as well as suspense, black comedy, offbeat romances with a sinister twist, and compromised relationships. In 1990 Sasaya won an Excellence Prize at the Japanese Cartoonists' Association awards for "Superior Observation by an Outsider." In 1996 she changed her personal name to Nanaeko and drew *Frozen Eyes*, a searing tale of child sexual abuse written by Atsuko Shiina that caused considerable controversy and had a follow-up series in 2003. Nanaeko Sasaya teaches at Kyoto Seika University's cartoon art department.

Keiko Takemiya

Keiko Takemiya has explored a variety of stories and themes, ranging from standard high school romances to BL, historical dramas, and hard sci-fi. Besides winning numerous awards for *To Terra* (also known as *Toward the Terra*), Takemiya is most notably credited as one of the key creators of the now hugely popular BL manga genre with her 1976 story, *The Poem of the Wind and Trees* (*Kaze to Ki no Uta*) and as a founding force behind *June*, a Japanese BL anthology magazine. Vertical has translated her sci-fi epics *To Terra* and *Andromeda Stories*, introducing her innovative work to English-

speaking audiences. Since 2000, Takemiya has been a professor at Kyoto Seika
University.

Mineko Yamada

Mineko Yamada made her debut in 1969
with *Haru no Uta*. In the 1970s, she began to draw for *Margaret*, then for *Hana
to Yuma*, and eventually for *Lala*. Her
most popular series is *Harmageddon*.
In the 1990s she also began to write
novels. Currently, she has withdrawn
from working in manga except for some
dōjinshi titles.

Ryoko Yamagishi

Rising through competition as a semi-
finalist in a 1966 contest sponsored by
Shōjo Friend, Ryoko Yamagishi made
her professional debut in 1968 with
"Left and Right," a short story that ran
in *Ribon*. Her works normally have oc-
cult themes, although her manga about
Russian ballet, *Arabesque*, and Kodansha
Manga Award–winning *Hi Izuru Tokoro
no Tenshi* are her most popular works. In
2007 she won the Grand Prize in the 11th
Annual Tezuka Osamu Cultural Prizes
for *Terpsichora* (*The Dancing Girl*).

Detail from the cover to the first volume of Keiko Takemiya's *The Poem of the Wind and Trees.*

(*Kaze to Ki no Uta*, Shogakukan, 2007–2008. Courtesy Frenchy Lunning.)

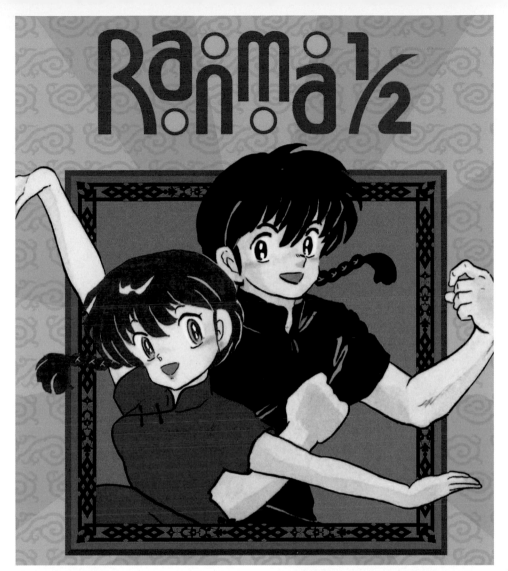

Cover detail from the
second volume of VIZ
Media's 2-in-1 Edition of
Ranma ½.

(*Ranma ½* ©1988 Rumiko Takahashi /
Shogakukan. Courtesy VIZ Media.)

RUMIKO TAKAHASHI

Mangaka

"Princess of Manga" Rumiko Takahashi has built a career around transcending gender boundaries. Taka-
hashi has created numerous award-winning series and inspired several

popular animated shows since she began publishing professionally in 1978, and she is one of the most successful mangaka in the world. As *Comics Alliance* writes, "Odds are if you've ever encountered anime or manga, you've seen something either by her or inspired by her. Her career has few equals in terms of proliferation and success" (2016).

Born in Nigata, Japan, Takahashi attended the college Gekiga Sonjuku, where she received guidance from legendary mangaka Kazuo Koike, the writer of *Lone Wolf and Cub* and *Crying Freeman*. Although she was repeatedly told that manga wasn't a woman's craft, the publication of her first professional story in the boys' magazine *Weekly Shōnen Sunday* earned her the 1978 New Comic Artist Award. "My parents said 'Don't do it, you won't be able to eat—get a normal job!'" recalls Takahashi in an interview with Toren Smith. She adds:

> And to be perfectly truthful, I myself wasn't absolutely sure I could do it... there was a lot of uncertainty in my own mind as to whether or not I'd be successful. And in fact, I ended up living in a roku-jo room [about 150 sq. ft.] along with my assistants. It was so crowded that I had to sleep in the closet! (1990)

Takahashi's most recognized work, *Ranma ½*, began in 1987. It follows the adventures of Ranma Saotome, a boy who has been trained in martial arts but is cursed to turn into a girl when splashed with cold water. He resumes his male form when splashed with hot water, and the series focuses on his adventures and mishaps as he tries to get rid of the curse. But Ranma is no simple victim of the curse; he often changes form willingly to accomplish something he desires. The series features other characters

who make similar transitions, often into animals. The manga and associated anime are among the first to find popularity in the United States. The series ended in 1996 with 38 volumes and more than 50 million copies sold in Japan alone.

Although her work has appeared primarily in boys' manga magazines and her inspirations include, amongst others, American superheros like the Fantastic Four, the Hulk, and Spider-Man, Takahashi's books appeal as much to girls as they do to boys. In fact, Takahashi points out that creating works for both boys and girls has always been a very conscious goal for her. "I'm not the type who thinks in terms of societal agendas," Takahashi said in a 1993 interview with Seiji Horibuchi for *Animerica*, but she was delighted with the series' popularity with girls.

In 1980, Takahashi won the highly prestigious Shogakukan Manga Award for *Urusei Yatsura* and again in 2002 for *InuYasha*. She has become a beloved icon in her home country, but she's found adoration in the United States as well. In 1994, Takahashi was awarded the American Inkpot Award for the groundbreaking international contributions she has made as a mangaka. In 2014 and 2016 she was nominated for the Eisner Awards Hall of Fame.

FURTHER READING

Ranma ½ 2-in-1 Edition (multiple volumes) by Rumiko Takahashi (VIZ Media)

InuYasha VIZBIG Edition (multiple volumes) by Rumiko Takahashi (VIZ Media)

Rin-Ne (multiple volumes) by Rumiko Takahashi (VIZ Media)

Panel from "The Willow Tree," collected in Moto Hagio's *A Drunken Dream and Other Stories*.
(Published by Fantagraphics, 2010. Courtesy Fantagraphics.)

MOTO HAGIO
Mangaka

Hagio-sensei is the most well-known of the 24 Nengu-mi, the group of female mangaka of the late 1960s through the 1970s and beyond. These women kicked down the gendered door of comic art—which had been a musky bulwark of rigid patriarchy. But as these remarkable women began to crash the party, strange things began to happen to manga. There were more stories about emotion, love, and sex in its many manifestations; the characters gender-shifted; panels began mutating, breaking, and finally disappearing; a new symbology and code emerged, this time around feminine desire; and new kinds of stories appeared, with a new atmosphere—darker, deeper, riskier, and at times taboo.

Into this moment arrives a young woman who is at odds with her culture, her parents, and her expectations. It is with her mother that Hagio-sensei felt the first censuring voice. Her parents, but particularly her mother, disapproved of her work in manga. As she relates it: "Throughout my entire

Panel from *The Heart of Thomas*.
(Published by Fantagraphics, 2013. Courtesy Fantagraphics.)

career, my mother has scolded me, telling me to 'Stop doing this awful work'" (Aoki 2010).

Hagio-sensei's first long story, *The Poe Clan* (*Poe no Ichizoku*), serialized from 1972 to 1976, was a story about murder, vampires, incest, and the innocence of two children destroyed. Hagio-sensei's masterpiece of illicit desire and loneliness, *The Heart of Thomas* (*Thomas no Shinzou*), began shortly after in 1973 and introduces homosexual love between schoolboys. Thanks to the more daring marketing policy at Shogakukan, Hagio-sensei was not censored in this radical manga, but there were low expectations in terms of its success. As she remembers:

> Once *Heart of Thomas* began, the editor

told me, "End it quickly." Then a miracle occurred. *The Poe Clan* was published in paperback format. *The Poe Clan* was the very first shojo manga from Shogakukan Publishing to be published in this new (at the time) tankobon format. The first print run was 30,000 copies; it sold out in one day. The publisher then said, "Well, maybe you can continue this story a little longer." (Aoki 2010)

Hagio's longest-running series, *A Cruel God Reigns* (*Zankokuna Kami ga Shihai suru*, 1992–2001), which tells the story of a boy abused by his stepfather, won the first Osamu Tezuka Cultural Prize Award for Excellence in 1997. Her 2003–2005 sci-fi series *Otherworld Barbara* was awarded the Japan SF Grand Prize in 2006. In Hagio-sensei's more recent work, she explores critical contemporary issues. In the short story, "Nanohana" (2012), Hagio-sensei examines how the relationship of humans to the natural world might be reconsidered.

Moto Hagio has emerged as a tireless and exceptional artist whose works, despite the many efforts to dissuade her, have resulted in her name being known around the world—not just as part of the remarkable 24 Nengumi, not just for her steadfast feminism—but as a mature, dedicated artist whose work is profound, complex, philosophical, critical, and very beautiful.

FURTHER READING

Otherworld Barbara by Moto Hagio (Fantagraphics, 2016)

The Heart of Thomas by Moto Hagio (Fantagraphics, 2013)

A Drunken Dream and Other Stories by Moto Hagio (Fantagraphics, 2010)

MACHIKO HASEGAWA

Mangaka

Creator of the popular long-running comic strip *Sazae-san*, Machiko Hasegawa remains one of Japan's most beloved manga artists.

One of the first female mangaka, Hasegawa has been named the "grandmother of manga" (*The Beat* 2006), had a museum founded in her honor, and inspired many generations of creators, men and women alike. Her works celebrated a more liberal woman in postwar Japan, and Hasegawa's cartoons brought a sense of humor and levity to everyday life. She was one of the most successful female cartoonists in the manga industry. Upon her death in 1992, Japan's *Asahi Shimbun* called Hasegawa the "greatest Japanese cartoonist since the equally popular Tezuka Osamu [*Astro Boy*]" (Kirkup 1992).

Born in 1920 in Saga Prefecture, Hasegawa got her start in cartoons at the young age of 26, drawing the first *Sazae-san* strips in 1946. Centered around the everyday bustle of housewife and mother Sazae-san, the comic tells the story of ordinary life in postwar Japan. The strip recounts the adventures of

The closest Western analog for *Sazae-san* in terms of content and popularity is Charles M. Schulz's *Peanuts*.

* Coming-of-Age Day (Seijin no Hi) is a national holiday that falls on January 15 and celebrates young people reaching the age of 20.

Sazae-san and her family with wry humor and wit. As James Kirkup describes the series:

> Critics and sociologists compared Sazae-san with Blondie but there is no similarity, for Sazae-san is no feather-pated stay-at-home, but a highly articulate, active mother and housewife. The strip is more like *Peanuts* crossed with *Denis [sic] the Menace*, with an often very moving loyalty to traditional family values and warm-hearted neighbourliness of a kind now almost non-existent in Japanese cities. (1992)

In 1949, after three years of publication in a local paper, Hasegawa's talent was recognized by the prestigious *Asa-hi Shimbun*. She was hired to produce an ongoing four panel *Sazae-san* comic exclusively for the newspaper. "Machiko was the originator of the now basic four-panel cartoon, and her success inspired a host of women cartoonists to enter a field until then dominated by men," wrote Kirkup in his obituary of Hasegawa (1992).

In 1955, *Sazae-san* was adapted into a radio series. In 1969, it became a weekly animated television show, which still runs today and holds the Guinness World Record as the longest-running animated TV series. Nearly 7,500 individual episodes (three per week) have aired. *Sazae-san* also has been adapted into multiple live-action series.

The strip ran until 1974, with an impressive 45 volumes of cartoons seeing print. Hasegawa would infuse a sense of feminine strength into the cartoon, a reflection of Hasegawa herself, who never married and was staunchly protective of the *Sazae-san* copyright—both considered unusual characteristics for a woman in Japan.

Hasegawa was given the People's Honour Award in 1992. The indelible mark she left on Japanese culture and manga can still be felt today. "Hasegawa's art is simple and direct in its humor," writes *The Beat*. "Certainly it was an influence on such things as *Crayon Shinchan*—and her name should certainly be added to the list of the most successful female cartoonists of all time" (2006).

FURTHER READING

Sazae-san (multiple volumes) by Machiko Hasegawa (English-language editions released by Kodansha, 1997–1999)

Under Karen Berger's leadership, the Vertigo imprint would change the face of mainstream comics.

(Artwork by Brian Bolland. From *Vertigo: Winter's Edge* #1, January 1998. Vertigo © and ™ DC Comics. Courtesy DC Comics.)

KAREN BERGER
Modern Age • Editor

Dubbed the mother of "the weird stuff" by *The New York Times* (Itzkoff 2013), Karen Berger left an indelible mark on the mainstream comics industry. From modern masterpieces like *Y: The Last Man* and *Fables* to seminal classics like *Preacher*, *The Invisibles*, and *The Sandman*, Berger saw an opportunity to expand the comics universe into realms outside of Gotham City and Metropolis, shaping a space for creators to tell their own unique stories in the process. The result was a comics imprint that had no equal: Vertigo.

In 1979, fresh out of Brooklyn College with a degree in English literature and art history, Berger entered the offices of DC Comics looking for a job. An assistant to Paul Levitz, Berger recalls developing an interest not in the meat of DC's publishing line—the superhero fare—but in some of the off-beat horror and mystery titles DC had held onto in the aftermath of the Comics Code. "I was fortunate enough to have started at a time, 1979, when DC was still doing other things besides superhero comics," Berger told *Sequential Tart*'s Jennifer Contino. She continued:

> I could just never relate to them. I thought they were too male orientated. I did like the horror, mystery, and fantasy comics though. I was lucky I got my start editing those kinds of books. After six months into the job, I was editing *House of Mystery*. The work I did on that title was in many ways the seeds of how Vertigo really began.

With an eye for the weird and different, Berger edited DC's more fantasy and sci-fi oriented series like *Wonder Woman, The Legion of Superheroes, Amethyst,* and *Arion,* but her true editorial calling was in identifying and cultivating new talent under an imprint that would allow the sort of mature content that would never fit within the confines of the Comics Code. "We talked a lot about the creative direction of the titles and the impact that they had in the market," recalls Berger. "We decided to create a separate imprint for them, a rare thing to do in those days, and to actively expand this sensibility. I came up with a publishing plan for the imprint, the Vertigo name, and then we worked on acquiring many new projects" (Contino).

Under Berger's guidance, Vertigo launched in 1993. With a focus on creator-driven content, Vertigo helped launch the careers of some of the biggest names in comics, including Neil Gaiman (*The Sandman*), Grant Morrison (*The Invisibles*), and G. Willow Wilson (*Ms. Marvel*). "Vertigo is successful because of the many talented writers and artists who created so much quality material," Berger told Contino. "Paul and Jenette [Kahn] have given Vertigo a lot of freedom and allowed us to explore and do many controversial things."

Because of the flexibility in terms of content, the Vertigo imprint attracted new audiences and opened doors into library and education spaces. *The Sandman* in particular would help prove the relevancy of comics as literature. As Vertigo helped raise the status and visibility of comics, the mature content in some of the books would face challenges. Books like *Y: The Last Man* and *The Sandman* attracted the unwanted attention of censors and critics who couldn't wrap their minds around the ideas that comics are literature and they can be created with adult audiences in mind.

Berger left Vertigo in 2013. For more than three decades, she cultivated some of the most innovative books in the industry, and inspired a new generation in the process. Creators sought Berger out specifically. G. Willow Wilson, whose first comics work, *Cairo*, was published by Vertigo in 2007, explains: "As a young female writer in a very male-dominated industry, Karen was a such a wonderful role model, because she'd done it all" (Itzkoff 2013).

FURTHER READING

The Sandman (multiple volumes and editions) by Neil Gaiman and various artists (DC Comics)

Y: The Last Man (multiple volumes and editions) by Brian K. Vaughan and Pia Guerra (DC Comics)

Preacher (multiple volumes) by Garth Ennis and Steve Dillon (DC Comics)

The Dark Knight Returns,
published while Kahn
led DC, would promote
acceptance of comics as
literature.

(Artwork by Frank Miller and Lynn Varley.
Batman © and ™ DC Comics. Courtesy
DC Comics.)

JENETTE KAHN

Modern Age • Publisher

For 26 years, DC Comics was run by a woman who oversaw one of the company's most successful periods. The
success wasn't just in terms of revenue, but also in the expansion of what
comics were capable of and how they were perceived outside of the industry.

Jenette Kahn got her start in children's publishing. In 1975, Kahn was approached by Warner Communication's Bill Sarnoff, who asked her to be publisher for his failing comic book company, National Periodical Publications.
Kahn talked about her experience entering the male-dominated comics industry as the first female publisher at DC Comics:

The beginning was difficult. We basically manufactured male fantasy, and everyone who created those fantasies, they were men, too. There was a lot of fear and loathing that I had been hired. It was said that one of my all-time favorite editors was throwing up in the men's room when he heard about it. (MAKERS 2014)

One of the first things Kahn did was push for renaming the company. It had been known colloquially as DC Comics for years, but the name didn't become official until 1977, a year after Kahn began her tenure as publisher. In 1981, Kahn was promoted to president and editor-in-chief of DC Comics.

Beyond rebranding the company, Kahn realized that any revitalization of comics had to involve creators' rights:

I felt that there were artists and writers who had great ideas, and they were not bringing them to us. So, I went in to Bill Sarnoff, and I said, I believe we could be publishing many new titles, many great ideas, and what's standing in the way is that we don't share revenue. And that argument actually carried the day. (MAKERS 2014)

Kahn also changed the focus of books from plot-driven stories to character-driven stories. She was able to enlist Frank Miller, who at the time was finding large audiences writing and drawing for Marvel. The result included a book that helped change the face of comics: *The Dark Knight Returns*.

Kahn described the impact of *Dark Knight* and the comics that followed:

Dark Knight signaled a seismic shift. All the extraordinary books that have come after it, *Watchmen*, *The Killing Joke*, *Arkham Asylum*, *The Sandman*, *Preacher*, *Planetary*, *The Authority*, *100 Bullets* (and great books from other publishers,

too, like *American Flagg*) owe a debt to it. *Dark Knight* turned comics on its head... *Dark Knight* was more book than comic. Unlike magazines and other supposedly disposable ephemera, *Dark Knight* and the comics it made possible could take their place on the library shelf. (Contino)

Under Kahn's leadership, DC Comics also saw the launch of the Vertigo imprint, and she oversaw the addition of the short-lived but immensely influential Milestone imprint, which introduced something that comics sorely lacked: creators and characters of color. Kahn's emphasis on diversity also found a home in the fabric of DC Comics itself. When Kahn joined DC, she was one of three women in a staff of 35. By the time she left DC in 2002, the staff had increased to 250, and half were women.

Kahn wasn't just the first woman to lead a major comics publisher—she helped change the face of the medium. Under Kahn's 26 years of leadership, DC Comics subverted the self-censorship of the Comics Code, strengthened creator rights, and attracted a wider audience that included more women and people of color. Many of the titles that Kahn published proved that comics could be used to tell sophisticated stories and fostered unprecedented acceptance of comics as literature.

FURTHER READING

The Dark Knight Returns by Frank Miller, Klaus Janson, and Lynn Varley (DC Comics, 2016)

Watchmen by Alan Moore and Dave Gibbons (DC Comics, 2014)

Superman: The Death of Superman by various (DC Comics, 2016)

Detail from "Industry News and Review No. 6," Mouly's only cartoon for *RAW*.

(Published in *RAW* #1. ©1980 Françoise Mouly. Used with permission.)

FRANÇOISE MOULY

Modern Age • Publisher & Editor

From her underground work to her current roles as comics publisher and art editor, Françoise Mouly has become a driving force in publishing. "Françoise has been one of the most influential people in comics for 30 years," Peggy Burns, associate publisher Drawn & Quarterly, told *Maclean's* magazine (Kingston 2013). As the co-founder of the groundbreaking *RAW* magazine, the publisher and editorial director of Toon Books, and art editor at *The New Yorker*, Mouly has consistently fought for the legitimization of comics as art as well as speech protected by the First Amendment.

Born in Paris in 1955, Mouly studied architecture at the prestigious École Nationale Supérieure des Beaux-Arts. She moved to the U.S. in 1974 and soon met Art Spiegelman, who would become her husband and frequent creative partner. In those early days, she was surprised at the drastically different prevailing attitude towards comics in this country. Whereas in Europe the comics industry had cultivated a rich and respected history, from the production of high-class satire magazines like *Punch* to classic comics like *Astérix* and *The Adventures of Tintin*, in the United States creators were still struggling to find avenues for their works and were frequently censored by the still-imposed Comics Code.

Looking to provide a home for high-brow experimental comics that could elevate the art form in the U.S., Mouly and Spiegelman founded *RAW* magazine in 1980. Printed on heavy paper stock using high-quality ink, each oversized issue featured custom embellishments such as pasted-in illustration cards and covers artfully ripped by hand. The couple produced 11 issues in as many years, albeit on an irregular schedule, and became a primary stateside conduit for alternative comics. *RAW* also hosted the serialized version of Spiegelman's *Maus*, which was collected in 1991. *Maus* later won the Pulitzer and became one of the first American graphic novels to be widely collected in libraries and studied in classrooms.

In 1993 Mouly became art editor at *The New Yorker*, a position she still holds today. She successfully brought the publication back to its artistic roots and introduced a wider audience to comics artists such as Sue Coe and Robert Crumb. During her tenure, the magazine has frequently featured covers that are iconic and sometimes provocative. Perhaps most memorable are the post-9/11 cover featuring black-on-black Twin Towers, which she credited to Spiegelman although it was a collaborative effort, and Barry Blitt's 2008 cover of Barack and Michelle Obama bumping fists, which satirized the various racial and xenophobic anxieties that bubbled to the surface during that year's presidential campaign.

Mouly has also brought her meticulous editing skills and comics advocacy to children's books, first with the RAW Books imprint Little Lit in 2000

and then with the separate press Toon Books in 2008. Prior to establishing Toon Books herself, Mouly recalls in a *Smithsonian* interview, she had been disappointed in her efforts to interest publishers in the idea of high-quality children's comics:

> I saw that the educational system was prejudiced against comics. I went to see every publishing house and it was a kind of circular argument. It was like, "Well, it's a great idea, but it goes against a number of things that we don't do." (MacGregor 2015)

Instead, Mouly struck out on her own with Toon Books for beginning readers and met with such critical and popular success that in 2014 she added a middle-grade imprint, Toon Graphics. This is just the latest example of her publishing instincts proving true, she told *Smithsonian*'s Jeff MacGregor:

> All I know is, I know to trust [myself], and that has served me well. If I see something, how something could be, I should go out and do it. I shouldn't ask permission from anybody. The thing to stay away from, for me, is what unfortunately is too often the case in publishing, that they all want to publish last year's book. I want to publish next year's book! The book of the future.

FURTHER READING

Blown Covers: New Yorker Covers You Were Never Meant to See by Françoise Mouly (Abrams Books, 2012)

In Love with Art: Françoise Mouly's Adventures in Comics with Art Spiegelman by Jeet Heer (Coach House Books, 2013)

Outside the Box: Interviews with Contemporary Cartoonists by Hillary L. Chute (University of Chicago Press, 2014)

Cover detail from *Sin City: Hell and Back* #1 one of the Frank Miller titles that Schutz edited.

(Published July 1999. Artwork by Frank Miller. Sin City © and ™ Frank Miller Inc. Courtesy Dark Horse Comics.)

DIANA SCHUTZ
Modern Age • Editor

Editor, writer, educator, and advocate **for creators' rights, Diana Schutz has become a venerable icon in the industry.** For over three decades, Schutz has helped shape modern comics and laid the foundation for its future. Now retired from her position as executive editor of Dark Horse Comics, Schutz nonetheless helped open mainstream comics to independent, creator-owned works.

Schutz got her start in comics at the ground level in 1978, working at Vancouver-based store The Comicshop, where she was one of the few female employees and customers. Mainstream comics of the time focused on male readers and were made up primarily of superhero books, but Schutz discovered underground comix and the independent works of Dave Sim (*Cerebus*)

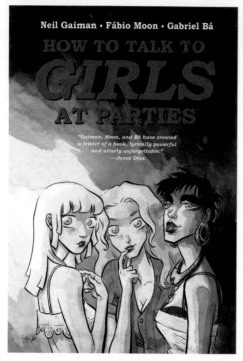

Neil Gaiman • Fábio Moon • Gabriel Bá

HOW TO TALK TO
GIRLS
AT PARTIES

"Gaiman, Moon, and Bá have created
a triolet of a book, lyrically powerful
and utterly unforgettable."
—Junot Díaz

taken for granted back then as they are now. Many of us felt very strongly that creators had not been getting treated properly by the corporate superhero publishers. So, it was politically important to us to go with Dark Horse because of the company's stance towards creators and the opportunities it offered creators. (Campbell 2015)

Schutz would edit some of the publisher's biggest projects, including Frank Miller's *Sin City* and work by comics legends such as Will Eisner, Harvey Pekar, and Neil Gaiman. She would also found the company's short-lived but impactful Maverick imprint, which focused on creator-owned work.

When she retired from her position at Dark Horse in 2015, Schutz didn't stop working in the industry. Schutz still edits, and she now teaches a new generation of fans about comics at Portland State University. Schutz offers the following insight:

I see more and more women now entering the field, and one result of women making publishing decisions is that there are more reading choices for women than ever before, which continues to bring more women in, and so the one feeds the other. Things have definitely changed since 1978 and my first day on the job at The Comicshop, when a customer asked the owners, "Who's the skirt?" (Campbell 2015)

and Wendy and Richard Pini (*Elfquest*) while working at Comicshop.

After leaving Comicshop, Schutz worked on the newsletter/fanzine *The Telegraph Wire Comics & Comix* in Berkeley, California; had a very short stint as an editor at Marvel; and became editor-in-chief at Comico, where she worked on Matt Wagner's *Grendel*. In 1989, Schutz made the move to Dark Horse, where she would make her biggest impact as an advocate for creators' rights. "Mike Richardson founded Dark Horse on the principle of creators' rights," notes Schutz, adding:

The company paid royalties and offered ownership to writers and artists; these were all political ideals that were really important in the industry and weren't

FURTHER READING

Sin City (multiple volumes and editions) by Frank Miller (Dark Horse Comics)

How to Talk to Girls at Parties by Neil Gaiman, Gabriel Bá, and Fábio Moon (Dark Horse Comics, 2016)

Grendel: Devil Child by Diana Schutz and Tim Sale (Dark Horse Comics, 2008)

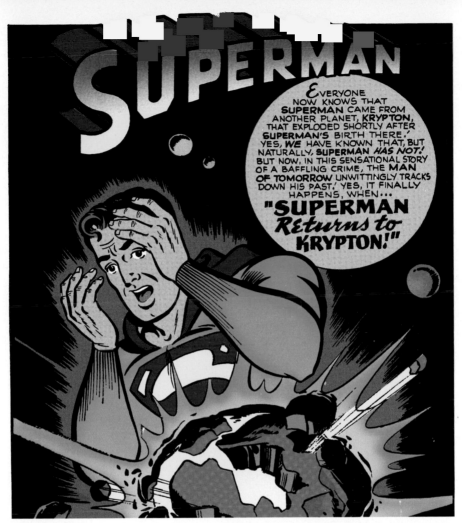

Thanks to Woolfolk, "Superman Returns to Krypton" introduced kryptonite as Superman's Achilles heel.

(From *Superman* #61, November 1949. Artwork by Al Pastino. Colors by Tom Ziuko. Superman © and ™ DC Comics. Courtesy DC Comics.)

DOROTHY WOOLFOLK

Golden Age & Silver Age • Editor

One of the first female editors in the comics industry—and the first at DC Comics—Dorothy Woolfolk was an **all-around innovator.** From the marquee title *Superman* to DC's internally-neglected and disparaged romance line, Woolfolk was known for carefully fostering fresh talent. In the face of rampant sexism, she helped ensure the survival of the format by bringing new ideas and creators into the fold.

In the 1940s, Woolfolk edited books from various comics publishers, including All-American Publications (one of the companies that later merged to form DC), Timely Comics (predecessor to Marvel), and EC. During that era, she was an assistant editor on *Wonder Woman* and also wrote some storylines, making her the first woman to write for the Amazonian heroine. By the late 1940s, Woolfolk would also become the first woman to become a full editor at DC.

One of Woolfolk's most notable contributions to comics is the concept of kryptonite as Superman's weakness. Woolfolk correctly perceived that a completely invulnerable hero would become boring, so she pushed for a regular plot device that could render Superman defenseless. Kryptonite had been introduced in the radio serial in 1943, and it made the leap to comics under Woolfolk's guidance in *Superman* #61 (1949).

While raising her children in the 1950s and 1960s, Woolfolk concentrated on writing outside of comics, including some stories for the science fiction magazine *Orbit*. In 1971 Woolfolk returned to DC as the editor of their romance line, including *Falling in Love, Girls' Love Stories, Girls' Romances, Heart Throbs, Secret Hearts, Young Love,* and *Young Romance*. While many of her male colleagues looked down on the titles, historian Tim Hanley says she transformed the line as it "began to explore feminist themes, featuring protagonists with more agency who refused to settle for boys who didn't treat them properly" (2016).

In 1972 Woolfolk got the chance to do the same for a DC icon when she took over editing of *Superman's Girl Friend, Lois Lane*. Lois had always been a career woman, but under Woolfolk's tenure, she quit the *Daily Planet* and became her own boss. Lois also broke up with Superman, telling him she was "no longer the girl you come back to between missions" (Hanley 2016), and moved in with three female roommates, who joined in her adventures. Of course Superman still made regular appearances, but instead of constantly rescuing Lois, he now fought alongside her.

Lois' radical transformation only lasted seven issues, however, as Woolfolk was ousted from the title and then from DC altogether. Although then-editor-in-chief Carmine Infantino claimed it was because her books were late, Hanley points out that every one of her issues came out on time and Woolfolk even "successfully transitioned several titles from six or eight issues a year to monthly series" (2016). Writer, penciller, and friend Alan Kupperberg recalled a pattern of poor behavior:

> The "boys' club" always snickered behind [Woolfolk's] back. "Ding-a-ling," "Wolfgang," "Dotty Dorothy," and worse. Outside of the obvious basic sexism at play at 'all-male' DC, I think another reason Dorothy was not very respected comes back to the 'no running in the halls at DC' mentality. (2016)

Woolfolk never returned to comics, but she continued to advocate for women in the medium. Thankfully, such overt sexism has been expunged from DC Comics, but there is no doubt that Woolfolk struck one of the first blows for women in comics.

FURTHER READING

The Greatest Golden Age Stories Ever Told
by various (DC Comics, 1990)

Atena Farghadani with the artwork that led to her arrest and imprisonment.
(From the artist's Facebook page.)

ATENA FARGHADANI
Formerly Imprisoned • Cartoonist

Despite being jailed for her art, Iranian cartoonist Atena Farghadani remains a strident and outspoken voice for women's rights in her home country and beyond.

Farghadani was first arrested in August 2014 for her cartoon mocking members of Iran's Parliament as they debated a bill to ban voluntary sterilization procedures, such as vasectomies and tubal ligations, in an effort to reverse Iran's falling birthrate. But even before her arrest, she was already well-known to the government for her fearless advocacy on behalf of political prisoners, Baha'i minorities, and the families of protesters killed after the country's presidential election in 2009.

When Farghadani was released on bail while awaiting trial, she promptly uploaded a video to YouTube detailing abuses she suffered in prison, including beatings, strip searches, and nonstop interrogations. She was rearrested in January 2015 and was eventually convicted of "counter-revolutionary activity; undermining national security; insulting the Supreme Leader, the Iranian president, Members of Parliament and jail officials; and for spreading propaganda against the Islamic Republic" (CRNI 2016). She received the draconian sentence of 12 years and 9 months after a perfunctory jury-less trial led by a judge known to be particularly tough on political prisoners.

During Farghadani's appeal, she was additionally charged with "non-adultery illegitimate relations" for shaking her lawyer Mohammad Moghimi's hand. Contact between unrelated members of the opposite sex is technically illegal in Iran, but rarely prosecuted. Moghimi was also charged, and both parties could have received sentences of up to 99 lashes if convicted. Both were acquitted in January 2016, but in the course of the investigation, Farghadani was subjected to involuntary virginity and pregnancy tests. The former is carried out by physically checking for the presence of a hymen and is recognized by the World Health Organization as a form of sexual violence.

The forced exams were originally reported by Farghadani herself in a note to her family from prison, but the Iranian government confirmed that they did take place in a United Nations report. Ironically, Iranian officials claimed that "prison authorities carried out tests to respond to allegations of sexual assault against her on some websites" (Amnesty International 2016).

In April 2016, Farghadani's sentence was reduced on appeal from the original 12 years and 9 months to the 18 months she had already served. She was set free on May 3 and was greeted by family and supporters bearing flowers upon her exit from Evin Prison. Farghadani told Cartoonists Rights Network International that "although she's happy to be free, she is also concerned about all of the unknown prisoners who have no supporters." While other Iranian cartoonists under duress have fled the country when they could, Farghadani said that her hope is "to stay in Iran and continue working as an artist" (CRNI 2016).

Indeed, mere weeks after her release, Farghadani was back to creating and posting editorial cartoons and speaking out online. In a short video she sent to the Facebook activist page *My Stealthy Freedom*, where Iranian women post pictures of themselves without hijabs, she said: "Some people think that art is not important, but the responsibility of an artist is to challenge authority and to be challenged. Sometimes the price for an artist is imprisonment, but do not forget that artists have responsibilities" (2016). Farghadani also expressed her commitment to staying in Iran despite the risk of imprisonment in an interview with *The Washington Post*: "As long as I live, I will stay here, even if I have to go to prison again" (Cavna 2016).

The depiction of Adam in this cartoon purportedly led to threats and a Muslim Brotherhood–backed lawsuit against Eladl.
(©2012 Doaa Eladl)

DOAA ELADL
Threatened • Cartoonist

Refusing to bow to the increasing pressure placed upon political cartooning in Egypt, Doaa Eladl stood resolute against attempts to censor her work. As one of the few female cartoonists in the country, she has been both a key voice for women as the nation shapes its future and a prime target of fundamentalists, who would prefer that women remain silent.

In 2013, Eladl faced a Muslim Brotherhood–backed lawsuit alleging that one of her cartoons was blasphemous. According to Luiz Sanchez of *The Daily News Egypt*, "The cartoon depicts Adam and Eve standing beneath an apple tree on a cloud. Before them stands an Egyptian man with angel wings and a halo, who declares the couple would have never been expelled from heaven had they voted in favour of the [constitutional] referendum" (2012).

The lawsuit was filed against Eladl by Khaled El-Masry, the Secretary-General of the National Centre for Defence of Freedoms. Adam is considered a prophet in the Muslim faith, and El-Masry declared, "the portrayal of prophets is a red line that we will not tolerate being crossed." Eladl refused to back down in the face of the suit, criticizing those who brought it and warning, "Artistic freedom in Egypt is being attacked, and this will send Egypt backwards fast" (Sanchez 2012).

The lawsuit evaporated with the Mohamed Morsi presidency, but Eladl's critics didn't back down. Speaking to *Sampsonia Way*, she explained, "Explicit threats against me and the cartoons I publish on social networks are still being expressed and have even increased in ferocity. Such threats have become commonplace these days and are experienced by many journalists and cartoonists in these turbulent times in Egypt"(Stransky 2013).

Despite the threats, Eladl continued to speak out against abuses, notably with a cartoon protesting female genital mutilation—still widely practiced in Egypt despite being outlawed in 2008—with a drawing of a man snipping a red flower from between a woman's legs. The graphic symbolism shocked many readers, but Eladl told Stransky that she is pleased to have jump-started a conversation about the practice:

> The subject of female genital mutilation has not been handled in such a direct way before. Some readers liked the idea behind the cartoon and were motivated to demand an end to this crime, while others attacked the cartoon and rejected my decision to deal with the issue. I believe that these strong reactions to the cartoon is a good thing, whether the reaction is acceptance or rejection. (2013)

Although her career path has not been easy, Eladl is determined to keep drawing what she feels and is gratified that many Egyptians do appreciate her cartoons. She tells *Sampsonia Way* that the difficulties she's faced have only strengthened her resolve:

> In the beginning of my career as a female cartoonist, I faced lots of obstacles. It was rare to find a woman who drew political caricatures. Colleagues of my generation used to disregard my abilities, and when I first started drawing, senior cartoonists thought that I was going to quit in a short time. However these obstacles made me determined to carry on. After several years, I finally succeeded in my field, and I have my own audience, which doesn't care if I am male or female. (2013)

Eladl continues to speak out, with her cartoons for *Al Masry Al Youm* appearing frequently online at *Cartoon Movement* (www.cartoonmovement.com).

female genital mutilation

15

The practice of female genital mutilation is one of the many topics Eladl addresses in her work.

(©2013 Doaa Eladl.)

*THIS IS AN ORGANIZATION CREATED INSIDE THE TOKYO POLICE THAT CONDUCTS RESEARCH SPECIFICALLY FOR THE POLICE DEPARTMENT.

ROKUDENASHIKO

Prosecuted for Obscenity • Mangaka

In 2014, Japanese artist Megumi Igarashi was arrested and jailed under obscenity charges in her native country for distributing 3D plans of her own genitals on the internet. The plans were among the premiums in a crowdfunding campaign to raise money for her project to construct a "vagina kayak."

Igarashi, who works under the pseudonym Rokudenashiko, or "good-for-nothing girl," creates art challenging sexism and cultural attitudes about nudity. A self-described "*manko* (vagina) artist," Igarashi writes in *What Is Obscenity?*, her 2016 manga memoir about her experiences:

There is something wrong when what amounts to an organ in everyone assigned female at birth is approached with such overdetermined derision or special treatment... Since I've started my work in *manko* art, I've been fighting back against the old men who complain about it.

With *manko* as her subject matter, Igarashi's art includes sculptures, drawings, and 3D-printed objects. As the result of a crowdfunding campaign to finance the creation of a kayak based on a digital scan of her genitals, Igarashi was arrested under obscenity charges. Igarashi was jailed for six days in July 2014, as charges were brought. A vast team of legal experts assembled to aid her case. In December 2014, she was arrested for a second time along with gallery owner Minori Kitahara for "obscene display," "digital distribution of obscene materials," and "digital distribution of obscene media." She was detained for 20 days, and only released after her legal team proposed bail of 1.5 million yen (approximately $15,000).

In a statement made to the Tokyo District Court, Igarashi spoke to the heart of her artistic practice:

> ...my work is motivated by concerns as to why the word "*manko*" is so problematic. It is nothing more than a part of my body, but mere utterance of these syllables, "ma-n-ko" causes outrage and fear. The equivalent word for genitals on men—*chinko* (penis, dick)—is used freely, but a celebrity who utters "*manko*" on television will be censored and barred from the program. I believe this is wrong... Using my anger as a springboard, I have made cheerful, positive *manko* art. (Rokudenashiko 2016)

In May 2016, Igarashi was found guilty of the distribution charge, and fined 400,000 yen (about $3,667). She was acquitted on a separate obscenity charge for displaying small plaster models of her vagina in a Tokyo sex shop. Because the models were not for sale and brightly painted such that they "did not obviously resemble female genitalia" (McCurry 2016), judge Mihoko Tanabe ruled that they were art and not obscene.

In 2016, CBLDF participated in an effort to ensure Igarashi's safe travel and admission to the U.S. and Canada during a tour in support of her memoir recounting her trial and imprisonment.

Excerpt from *What Is Obscenity?*, describing Igarashi's experience in jail with characteristic humor.

(*What Is Obscenity?*, p. 46. ©2016 Rokudenashiko. Courtesy Koyama Press.)

FURTHER READING

What is Obscenity? The Story of a Good for Nothing Artist and Her Pussy by Rokudenashiko (Koyama Press, 2016)

Bell's *El Deafo* was the first graphic novel to be shortlisted for the prestigious Newbery Medal.
(From *El Deafo*, p. 45. ©2014 Cece Bell. Courtesy Amulet Books / Abrams.)

CECE BELL
INTERVIEW • *Cartoonist*

The world of comics is full of characters who leverage unknown strengths to become heroic, but no one has lived that story quite like Cece Bell. Growing up deaf would've been an understandable challenge for any child, but Bell felt empowered by her differences. In her fictionalized memoir *El Deafo*, Bell not only gave voice to the insecurities that people with disabilities experience, but also invited readers of all abilities to understand those frustrations, proving that empathy is the greatest superpower of all.

How did you become interested in visual storytelling, and what sparked your love of comics?

When I was in the third grade, I was allowed to walk downtown by myself. My main stops were the drug store for candy, and the library. One day at the library, I discovered Ezra Jack Keats' book *The Snowy Day*, and it was the most amazing book I had ever seen in my young life. I'm still trying to make something that was as beautiful and pure as the words and pictures in Keats' book. My love of comics started around the same time, when I found this enormous, gorgeous collection of Winsor McCay's weekly comic masterpieces, *Little Nemo in Slumberland*. At this point, I had gone through a big pile of my cousin's superhero comics, but they didn't interest me the way *Little Nemo* did.

What are you seeing from your fans that's different from your early experiences with comics?

Kids are so much more knowledgeable than I ever was about, well, anything—not just comics. The total LOVE that they have for comics and writing and drawing is awe-inspiring. I don't think I had the same kind of intensity for books and popular culture that a lot of the fans have today, and I think that's partly because I didn't have access to my heroes the way young fans do today. Being able to communicate with the people who make the stuff you love—that's gotta be heady stuff for a kid.

In *El Deafo*, a girl, based on your young self, decides that what makes her different and could be perceived as a tragic disability instead makes

With *El Deafo*, Bell used her own experiences to help hearing people understand deafness and how to respectfully communicate with deaf people.

(El Deafo, p. 39. ©2014 Cece Bell. Courtesy Amulet Books / Abrams.)

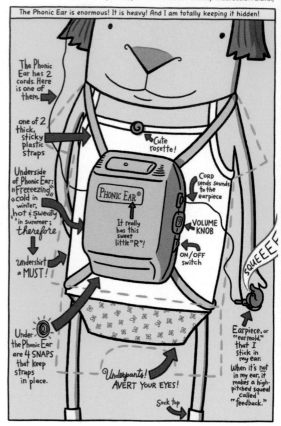

her powerful. What has the response been like from readers?

It has been surreal. The book seems to have touched a lot of people, because many, many people have experiences with deafness and hearing loss and hearing aids. I've heard from deaf kids and adults, as well as their friends and families and teachers.

The interactions melt my heart every time; I love finding out that my book helped this kid feel brave, and that kid feel proud. I've heard from kids who connected with the book even though they are not deaf—just about everyone feels different at some point in their lives.

Some of the most powerful interactions I've had, though, are with deaf adults who had very similar experiences as those featured in *El Deafo*. Often, they'll tell me that *El Deafo* is the first time they've really seen themselves in a book. It's as amazing to me as it is to them to find someone, and to talk to someone, who knows exactly how certain things feel. The book has a life of its own, and sometimes I feel like *El Deafo* no longer belongs to me—it belongs to everyone. Feeling different and trying to overcome that feeling is everyone's story, I think.

There's a growing sense that women are expected to do autobiographical and memoir work in a way that isn't assumed of men. Why do you think that is, and how do we overcome this misconception?

I think people assume that all women are able to—and want to—talk about their personal lives, and therefore the stories we want to tell and are good at telling are personal stories. That may be true for some of us, but obviously not for all of us. I don't necessarily mind this misconception. If a reader thinks that a story is based on someone's real life, that means the story rings true in some way, and therefore, it might be a more successful story.

One of the things that got many readers hooked on *El Deafo* was being shown how it felt to be a deaf child and how the world sounded to you. What would it have meant to you as a young reader to see a book like this?

I think I would have resisted it at first, simply because I had trouble accepting myself as deaf. I avoided any book that even touched on deafness, often because those books, while well-meaning, felt very patronizing and condescending to me.

I wanted to be as funny and honest as I could with *El Deafo*. I wanted to make a book that Kid Me would have wanted to read. I hope that if I had found a book like this as a kid, I would have locked myself in my room and read it again and again, and I would have been so relieved to discover that there were other people out there just like me who were doing just fine. Relieved is totally the right word.

As we see more and more female creators and characters telling their stories in comics, the landscape will continue to shift. What do you think comics will be like in five years, and what are your hopes for the future of the industry?

We're clearly living in a golden age of visual storytelling, and we're going to see more and more amazing comics by all kinds of talent. I think comics forge a deep and immediate connection between characters and readers in a way that "regular" books cannot, and therefore foster real empathy in readers. There can never be too much empathy in this world. I'd love to see everyone embrace comics, and I'd love for comics to be accessible to everyone.

FURTHER READING

El Deafo by Cece Bell (Amulet Books, 2014)

Campbell and writer Kelly Thompson have introduced different body types, people of color, and gender identities into *Jem and the Holograms*.

(Detail from *Jem and the Holograms*, #1 p. 20. JEM & THE HOLOGRAMS, and all related characters are trademarks of Hasbro and are used with their permission. ©2016 Hasbro.)

SOPHIE CAMPBELL
INTERVIEW • *Cartoonist*

When it comes to changing comics, female characters are just as important as the women creating them, and few have fostered a more diverse character landscape than **Sophie Campbell.** In everything from licensed properties like *Jem and the Holograms* to her stunning *Wet Moon* series, Campbell has advocated for realistic and unique body types and proven there is a market for authentic diversity in terms of characters and identity.

How has the comics industry changed since you've been part of it?

Social media is the first thing I think of—I've watched it become a big part of comics, both professionally and in fandom. That's probably one of the biggest changes. It's really connected professionals to each other, which makes me feel more like I'm part of a real community, and given fans and pros a direct connection, which is really fun but sometimes hazardous! I also like how social media has brought problems, like racism and sexism, in the industry into the spotlight, and people can discuss them with ease. To me, that's invaluable.

Who were some of the women that have inspired you during your career?

Becky Cloonan is probably the most important one. I still remember the first time I met her, sometime around 2002. She's still a good friend and was an early champion of my work and helped my career take off. I still look up to her. Others who have inspired me over the years are Amy Reeder, Michelle Silva, Jillian Tamaki, Mariko Tamaki, and Erin Watson. I tend to be inspired by people who have a lot of energy and enthusiasm; they always get me excited to do my own thing.

Your work tends to focus on young adult characters and is incredibly welcoming to new readers. How do you approach telling these stories?

I don't have a particular process. It's mostly about what's the most fun for me to write and draw, and the stories I'd personally like to read. I just do what feels most natural and fun, while at the same time trying to be responsible about the content of my work (with varying levels of success).

Your work focuses on characters many people would consider outsiders. How do you develop your characters? What kind of traits are important for you to showcase?

I like to write characters who aren't squeaky clean, who could be seen as likable or unlikable depending on the reader, like real people are. I try to develop them and portray them like real people as much as I can. That's probably the most important thing, even when the characters are in a fantasy or sci-fi setting—like my comic *Shadoweyes*, for example. And again, a lot of what goes into my characters is what's most fun and interesting for me to write and draw. I feel like I have to be having fun or be excited about the characters, even if they do something horrible. If I'm not excited about them, then the whole thing suffers.

I don't know if I have any traits that are important to me to portray. It really depends on the individual character. Even though my characters are usually definitely in my style and often have a similar look, I like having a range of personalities and body types and backgrounds as much as I can.

***Jem* has been an amazing example of embracing diversity. What was it like changing a licensed property? And why was it important for you to make those changes?**

It was remarkably easy doing the new *Jem* designs, the powers-that-be were very cool about it, and doing different body types is something I do anyway.

So, to me it wasn't anything out of the ordinary. I honestly didn't think about it too much—it's just what I do, and I applied that to *Jem*. It's always important to me to have SOME degree of varying body types even when I do licensed work-for-hire, and I felt doing that in *Jem* was maybe especially important because to me *Jem* is partly about diversity and different people coming together. They weren't really able to show that in the original cartoon and doll line, so I wanted to bring to *Jem* what I always felt the story and characters were about.

It's so much more common for women in comics to face censorship—how have you responded to challenges about your work?

I've had a few problems over the years with things that the powers-that-be don't like. It's almost always been things relating to the female characters' relative attractiveness. Like they think I draw a character too unattractive, too fat, too butch, too muscular, that sort of thing. We'll go back and forth about it. I try to roll with the punches and do what I can. I've gotten into a couple fights, but I try to pick my battles.

As comics continue to grow and evolve, what are your hopes for the future of the industry?

I hope the range of creators continues to grow as more and more new people enter comics, and I hope the airing of comics' dirty laundry continues on its current path and keeps improving the industry. Also: more money.

FURTHER READING

Jem and the Holograms, Vol. 1: Showtime by Kelly Thompson and Sophie Campbell (IDW, 2015)

Wet Moon (multiple volumes) by Sophie Campbell (Oni Press)

Campbell's *Wet Moon* brought diverse characters and body types to comics.
(Artwork of characters Cleo and Mara courtesy Sophie Campbell.)

KATE LETH

INTERVIEW • *Cartoonist*

Kate Leth's autobiographical comics, including her webcomic *Kate or Die*, explore intimate details of her life.

("Job Interview" ©2016 Kate Leth. Courtesy Kate Leth.)

In the relatively short time that Kate Leth has been in the comics industry, she has made an incredible impact. From her intimate, honest webcomic *Kate or Die*, to her outspoken advocacy for LGBTQ visibility, to founding a professional community of women comics retailers known as The Valkyrics, to her popular work at Marvel (*Patsy Walker, A.K.A. Hellcat!*), BOOM! Studios (*Adventure Time*), and Dynamite Entertainment (*Vampirella*), Leth is just getting started.

Since we are talking about women shaping the landscape of free expression in comics, who have been some of your influences, and what did you learn from them?

I think my earliest understanding of a woman creating comics was Lynn

Johnston's *For Better or For Worse*, honestly. I was really young. It wasn't something I actively thought about until I was in high school and college, when I started getting really into webcomics and realizing how many women were making them. I wanted to do it myself, but felt that my lack of formal art education was a barrier. When I discovered Kate Beaton, who majored in history and made comics just for fun that people really responded to... That was the first time I thought to myself, "I could do this."

Since your career began, what kinds of changes have you seen in terms of free expression in comics, especially with regard to women's voices?

I think it depends on the medium. Webcomics and self-published projects are filled with all kinds of voices you don't see represented in mainstream books. Spike Trotman, for instance, the publisher of the *Smut Peddler* anthologies, is one of the smartest and most progressive voices in this industry. She operates almost exclusively on crowd-funding and does unbelievable business. It's opened the doors for a lot of really important projects that publishers might have otherwise passed on to see production. Superhero books have a long ways to go, but there's an endless amount of incredible work being put out online and through non-traditional means. It's all getting better, inch by inch, because of the tireless work of all of us.

You've openly advocated for the visibility of LGBTQ characters, especially in young adult comics. Was there ever any fear about pushing this forward? How did you approach it?

I was nervous at first, of course, but I don't really know what else to do besides put myself into my work. The first kids' books I did, I tiptoed around things, but now I really push for those kinds of stories to have room to breathe and develop in my books. I'm not scared of it anymore; people who hire me know what they're getting. Still, I've had to fight for it, and I don't always win, but I keep trying. I had no stories where the queer characters got a happy ending (or even got to be fully-realized, or god forbid, romantic!) when I was growing up, so I'm trying to make them for kids and young people now.

Your early work on *Kate or Die* was incredibly personal—what did that kind of free expression teach you? How did that shape you as a creator?

Kate or Die was this kind of necessary catharsis. I started it as an outlet, in lieu of therapy, for me to talk about things I had a hard time articulating. The art that means the most to me is the stuff that's honest, even when it's hard. Especially when it's hard. It made sense to me to do the same. Over time I had to step away from it as it felt less safe to be as honest, but I can't ever stop completely. That connection is the most rewarding part of creating. Now I do it in different ways, through fiction or in smaller doses.

Because of your outspokenness, you've also taken some criticism, particularly from voices on the internet. How do you fortify yourself for that? And how do you decide which voices matter?

When I started, I was a very sensitive 21-year-old, and so I felt like every criticism was an attack. A lot of them were, to be fair, but some of them were valid. I've said some stupid things, some insulting things, and my shield was up so high that the voices of people actually hurt by it just bounced off. I've gotten better at finding the balance, and listening to those voices. I don't pay attention to people who call me a feminazi or tell me to die, but I do listen to those who feel hurt by something I've written. The trouble is that so many creators, especially young ones, get chased out of the scene before they get a chance to find that balance. I would tell anyone wanting to make comics to really try and differentiate between the two—oh yeah, and turn off anonymous comments! You will inevitably screw up, but listen, learn, apologize, be genuine, and honestly strive to do better.

You founded one of the most incredible communities in comics—The Valkyries. How has that shaped the voice of women in the comics industry? What changes do you continue to push for?

The Valkyries are incredible to me. We're over 550 members strong and growing all the time! It's an incredible network and resource for women and non-binary / genderqueer folks to talk about comics, share stories, help each other, and better this industry. I think the most important thing it's done so far is give a voice to all these retailers, to unify them so that people really do pay attention. It's harder to dismiss the concerns of one person when she's got hundreds standing at her side, and there's a great deal of value in that. As for what we

Leth founded The Valkyries to support "the women behind the counters of comic shops worldwide."
(©Kate Leth, 2013–2016. Courtesy Kate Leth)

want to do, I think we want to continue to push for better representation both in characters and creators, and diversity in the Valkyries themselves, which starts with retailers and owners being more mindful of their hiring practices. We have a long way to go, but we're doing what we can.

What kind of legacy do you think your work will leave behind? And what are your hopes for the future generations of creators?

I have no idea! If anything, I hope someone out there sees what I'm doing and knows that it's possible, like Beaton's work did for me. I'm lucky enough to be in a place where I can be vocal, can be visibly queer, and still successful. This industry needs more of that, and I hope that as the stubborn older generation moves on, we see a lot more diverse creators getting their chance to show their stuff. I can't wait for that tide to turn.

FURTHER READING

Fresh Romance, Vol. 1 by various (Oni, 2016)

Patsy Walker, A.K.A. Hellcat!, Vol. 1: Hooked On A Feline by Kate Leth and Brittney Williams (Marvel, 2016)

Vampirella by Kate Leth and Eman Casallos (Dynamite Entertainment, 2016)

In this cartoon, which translates to "The road is (still) so long," Merhej illustrates the obstacles Arab cartoonists face.
(Courtesy Lena Merhej.)

LENA MERHEJ
INTERVIEW • *Cartoonist & Editor*

After a five-year court battle, the Lebanese indie comics collective Samandal was financially crippled after three of its editors were fined a total of $20,000 in 2015. They were charged with "a) inciting sectarian strife b) denigrating religion c) publishing false news and d) defamation and slander" (Samandal 2015). Lena Merhej, an artist and editor for the collective, wasn't fined, but she drew one of the offending cartoons.

What are the unique characteristics of Arab comics as you see them?

I wouldn't say that there's yet a characteristic. Right now it's really individual, like small interventions. *Samandal*, in the end, is a space for these artists to experiment, to learn, or to discover something new.

So, let's discuss your own interventions—could you tell us about your work?

I studied graphic design. A lot of women study graphic design, it's not considered a manly profession here. A manly profession would be engineering, architecture, law, medicine. Most visual designers are women. This made it that a lot of women also are doing comics.

My chapters in *Samandal* are about my mother. It was like a therapy—a discovery of where my anger was coming from, how can I live with it. I looked at my mom, at her anger, at the struggle of living in her country at war with many children and how she managed to somehow give us a window to something else. But also how war continues down the generations, how it's passed.

War is very abstract for American audiences because it's not something that touches our shores. Could you describe what the common experience of war is for your generation of Lebanese creators?

You're in a state of emergency. You don't think of anything else but your safety and other people's safety. There is this fear.

I was a child when there was war here. It was definitely scary, but not as scary or dramatic as my parents lived it. They were losing everything. They were responsible for five kids and had to keep them secure, but also to keep them educated. To give them a kind of normalcy. This was the situation for everyone here. How do you create such a balance when you don't know if going today to work there will be a bomb?

Other than this, I mean, some days we didn't have school, so that was nice. Some months we didn't have school, and that was also nice. You would go to the shelter and play with the kids there, so you create some kind of a bond. In general, in the war people seek solidarity. They seek to be among the community, and find ways to deal if there's no water or electricity, how to cover the shelter. We were displaced many times from many houses. This kind of attachment you have to home is lost. I feel like in my mother's life there was a struggle somehow to find a home.

I was a teenager then when the war ended. We were finally seeing what was on the other side and recognizing ourselves in the other. That was a struggle. Unfortunately, it's still a struggle because there was a general amnesty that didn't seek justice for many people. There is a lot of pain still and a lot of open wounds.

You put some of those wounds into the work that ultimately led to a major censorship case. Would you talk about that, please?

In 2007, we decided on a collaboration under the theme "revenge." I wanted to make something that was funny, *Mad Magazine* style. I thought I would make some "Lebanese Recipes For Revenge" using the Lebanese swear words. By showing literally what the bad words said, what they meant, I would show how violent these recipes were because we were living in a country of violence. The swear words that I chose were "I want to break your head," "I want to shit on you," "I want to burn your religion," and "I want to bombard your life."

The first one, "I want to break your head": you take a glass, you cut it, you break it on the edge of the table, and then you break it on the head of one of the characters and this is how he dies. "Bombard your life": this is definitely something very specific to Lebanon. What is worse than bombarding your house? I put Israeli planes shooting some buildings and saying "We want to bombard your life!" The one in particular that was the problem was "I want to burn your religion." It's represented by two religious men: one with the cross and the other with an 'amāma, it's like a turban, and I set them on fire.

The other [cartoon in the case] was by Valfret, who is from Belgium. He was working on the story about a legionnaire who is faced by confusion with his sexuality and the violence he is ordered to do. He is completely angered by this absurdity, which pushes him at the end to curse one of the victims that was on the cross, which was actually in the story not a Christian cross. It was the cross used by Romans to crucify their victims, their invaded people. These were the comics in question.

What happened is that we were taken to court. A minister of the Catholic Church complained to General Security of the country, who basically sued *Samandal*. With that, we lost the case with a big amount of money.

And five years of your life, right?

Four and a half, yes. It was a lot of waiting and postponing. All in all it was maybe three hearings, but there was no testimony from us. It was just accusations.

So the substance of their arguments was that this is offensive?

They said this work was calling for sectarian conflict and that it was blasphemy. We were fined $20,000. Of course we all had to go and borrow money. This is the first thing. The second thing is the case was not on me personally. I had a German passport, I was not Lebanese. It was on Hatem [Imam], Omar [Khouri], and Fadi [Baki, a.k.a. FDZ]. For them, it was terrible because they cannot move the way they wish, and the police can stop them when they want. It was horrible. FDZ was not able to travel once. Hatem had more complications with something simple where he had a camera on a bike, and they stopped him and harassed him, and I think put him in jail.

Despite this, *Samandal* will continue. What are the risks and dangers that you're concerned about?

The only risk is the censorship. Dragging the artists to court and having them pay. I think that would be terrible. We would all be discouraged. Now on the other hand, our lawyer says it's also a matter of defending cases so that we can work on a law that is clear for the future generations. I don't know how many of us are willing to be martyrs.

FURTHER READING

Muqtatafa by various (Ninth Art Press, 2015)

Kanika Mishra uses cartooning to address violence against women in her native India.
(Courtesy Kanika Mishra.)

KANIKA MISHRA
INTERVIEW • *Cartoonist*

Combining the editorial cartoonist's credo of speaking truth about those in power with the viral strength of social media, Kanika Mishra has become a major voice in her native country of India. Millions follow her cartoons online, often cheering her assaults on injustice. But at the same time, Mishra has endured significant intimidation, including death threats and rape threats and censorship on Facebook, for speaking out against the government. She spoke to us about her struggle and inspirations.

When you started cartooning, what was it like for women generally and women cartoonists specifically in India? How has that changed over time?

After completing my MFA, I came to Delhi looking for a job. I occasionally worked as a cartoonist for magazines and newspapers, but never got a chance to work as an editorial cartoonist. I tried but was rejected many times. Maybe, I was not considered fit for this job because they thought that being a woman, I will not be able to tackle difficult political subjects. The atmosphere was never encouraging. There was no legacy of political women cartoonists before me.

I used that spare time to learn new skills, like graphic design software and animation. I started working on freelance jobs and almost forgot all about my dream of becoming a cartoonist. Then one day, out of the blue, *Karnika Kahen* happened. The response was tremendous. People absolutely loved the concept of India's first cartoon everywoman.

What was the impetus of your series *Karnika Kahen*?

When I [made] my first cartoon of the series, I never realized that before her, we had only common man characters in Indian political cartoons. "Karnika Kahen" means "Karnika Speaks." She speaks without fear on political and social issues. She is the voice of a common girl, who could be living in any part of India, a metro or an interior village. She speaks on rape culture, on kangaroo court decisions, on the patriarchal nature of Indian society. There are many girls who send me messages that *Karnika Kahen* is an inspiration, and they decided to go into journalism after reading

my story. It really feels great.

You have also received a great deal of criticism for your cartoons.

The atmosphere is still not encouraging for me as a woman cartoonist. A senior cartoonist publicly insulted me because he didn't agree with a cartoon I made about Prime Minister [Narendra] Modi. He said that I am not mature enough to make political cartoons. My cartoons are seen by millions on the internet, and I receive lots of congratulatory messages, but the irony is that no media house is ready to hire me. I don't earn any money from my cartoons and survive only because cartooning is the passion of my life.

You've received death threats for criticizing guru Asaram Bapu, who is on trial for the rape of a teenage girl. How did authorities respond? How did you protect yourself?

When I made cartoons on Godman Asaram, his followers made my life very difficult for almost six months. I was not able to go out from my home, my phone was ringing continuously, and on the other end, there were these abusers who were threatening me. They also hacked my email and Facebook account and stole vital information and threatened that they will misuse it. Then, I went to Cyber Crime Police Cell and the local police station. They suggested [to] me not to make cartoons until they catch the culprits. I can say that they were concerned but I refused to stop making cartoons. I didn't want to send this message to *Karnika Kahen* fans that I gave up in fear. I simply stayed at home, didn't come out for four months but kept drawing and posting my cartoons online.

How concerned are you about censorship in India? Do you feel the urge to censor yourself due to the threats and censorship you have faced?

Very much. Whenever I post a cartoon against the current regime or some particular leader, I face lots of abuses from their followers in my comment boxes and sometimes threats in my inbox. There are serious attempts to intimidate me. But as I said, *Karnika Kahen* means Karnika speaks, and she speaks without fear. It is not about me, it is about the common girl. So, no question of self-censorship for me. Fortunately, I have not faced any action from authorities against me [until] now. Maybe it is because I am very vocal about it, a hell-raiser! I extensively use social media to make people hear what I want to say.

How have the internet and social media helped you share your work?

In every way! I almost forgot my dream of becoming a cartoonist, and one day I put few of my cartoons on Facebook and Twitter without any plan. I did it just to vent my anger against Godman Asaram and our society, and suddenly everything changed. I can't thank social media enough for that. I am still not associated with any media house and completely dependent on the internet and social media to reach to my viewers.

Unfortunately, Facebook has started censoring lots of meaningful content. They recently censored one of my cartoons on rape. They always fail to remove an abusive comment but very

This cartoon, drawn in response to a controversial statement about rape made by Indian Minister Maneka Gandhi, was blocked by Facebook.
(Courtesy Kanika Mishra.)

easily remove meaningful content if it is against the regime because it doesn't match with their "community standards." They really need to do something about it.

What do you think the future looks like for women cartoonists in India and around the world?

I think it is very bright. In fact, it has to be, because women need to raise their voice. Only then, the change will come. They just need to express themselves. It could be through any medium but they need to tell society what they want. I want to tell society, specifically our Indian society, please don't tell women what to do. Don't stop them from what they are doing, they can take care of themselves.

Pretty in Ink

NORTH AMERICAN WOMEN CARTOONISTS
1896-2013

By Trina Robbins

Among Trina Robbins'
innumerable contribu-
tions to comics is her
dedication to preserving
the history of women in
the medium.

TRINA ROBBINS

INTERVIEW • *Cartoonist & Historian*

From publishing the first all-women comics anthology to writing definitive histories of women in comics,
few women have changed comics as much as Trina Robbins
has. Robbins didn't let the boys' club keep her down, and she helped found
one of the most influential anthologies of the underground, *Wimmen's Comix*. She's also one of the most respected historians in the business.

**What was your relationship with comics before you started making
them?**

I always read comics. I was the kid who read everything. I read every book
in the house, the back of the cereal cartons, and... comics. I discovered that
I could go to the corner candy store and buy a comic with my tiny little al-

lowance. There would be some parents who would be afraid: "Oh she's reading comics, she won't read any books," but I read everything that had words.

What was it like for women when you started making comics?

There weren't any! My first comics were published in the underground newspaper the *East Village Other*, and it didn't even occur to me that I was the only woman doing comics. It wasn't until the late '60s that I started noticing that there were an awful lot of men and at that point, the only women were me and Willy Mendes.

In 1968, the poet Ed Sanders had a place called the Peace Sign Bookstore, and he decided to have an exhibit of cartoonists. He invited all the guys who were doing underground comix to exhibit, but he did not invite me. So, that was like my first inkling. Around the same time, summer of 1969, there was a convention in New York with the first panel ever of underground comix. Phil Seuling, who put the show on, asked Roger Brand (he was an underground cartoonist) to organize it. Roger, sure enough, invited a bunch of guys and did not invite me. I got on because at some point I was in a room with both Phil and Roger, and I told them that I drew underground comix. Phil said, "Oh, I hate underground comix," and I said, "Well I draw this strip called *Panthea*," and he said "I love *Panthea*! That's the only underground comic I like!" And he said to Roger, "You have to have her on the panel!" So, what could Roger do? He agreed, and I was on the panel.

In December 1969 I came to San Francisco, and what I found out really fast was that I was just not being included. In the underground maybe someone might put out a comic that was entirely his, but mostly the way they would put out books is they would phone a bunch of guys, their friends, and say, "Hey, I'm putting out a book, you wanna contribute?" But no one phoned me and asked me to contribute. They were having parties at that point. Really cool people like Janis Joplin would show up, but I was never invited to those parties.

So, time to throw your own party?

That's what happened. Someone showed me an issue of *It Ain't Me, Babe*, which was the first women's liberation newspaper in the entire country. I phoned them, and we met at a Be-In in Golden Gate Park. I was wearing a t-shirt I had designed with this angry looking superheroine with her fist raised and under it, it said "Super Sister." They loved my shirt and invited me to contribute. Working with the *It Ain't Me, Babe* collective behind me, I felt strong enough that I could turn out a comic that was all women. And that was the first all-women comic book, *It Ain't Me Babe* comics.

And that led to *Wimmen's Comix*. Can you tell me how that came about?

That came two years later. *Wimmen's* was great. It really was a collective. We would make group decisions although the editor, of course, always had the last word. We solicited art, and almost immediately, people would start sending us stuff. It was incredible.

Why did you go into underground comics and not mainstream comics?

When I first got the idea of drawing comics, which was probably in 1965, Batman and Robin were on television, and Marvel was having its renaissance. It hadn't yet occurred to me that comics could be anything but superheroes. So, I tried to do kind of a psychedelic superhero—a scientist who would take some kind of drug that enables him to see through walls and stuff like that. I may have done two pages of it and then gave up because I'm not a superhero artist. It just didn't work! Then someone showed me a copy of the *East Village Other*, and it was amazing. It was freewheeling and kinda psychedelic, and it had comics! The sudden realization that you could do comics that were not superheroes, it was like: "Wow, this is what I wanna do!"

The undergrounds faced several issues with obscenity. Did you ever worry about your own work facing censorship?

The only time I ran into a problem was in the mid-70s. Denis Kitchen asked me to edit an all-women comic book. I came up with the name *Wet Satin* and picked the cream of the crop of women cartoonists to do their erotic fantasies. It was really a good, beautiful book, but Denis' printer refused to print it. He said it was pornography. Denis also published *Bizarre Sex*, which had really graphic stuff in it, and the same printer published that. He justified it by saying, "*Bizarre Sex* is satire, but this isn't satire."

So you think it was because it was a women's book?

Yes, of course it was! Men's sex fantasies are fine, women's are not.

In addition to your comics work you've done substantial histories of women in comics and cartooning. Why was it so important to you to tell those stories?

In the '80s and '90s I was tired of hearing editors and publishers saying, "Girls don't read comics. Women have never drawn comics," because I knew it wasn't true! I had grown up on comics, and I wasn't the freak in the classroom. Everyone read comics! I just had to prove that these guys were wrong. I wound up researching women cartoonists and found that there were hundreds of them, and they had been really good and talented and prolific. Some of them, like Nell Brinkley, Tarpé Mills, Grace Drayton—these women were famous! And yet they were completely forgotten because nobody wrote about them.

What's your take on comics today?

Oh, it's wonderful! For women, the whole situation has never been better. You go down to the floor of the convention and see all those women sitting there and selling their comics—it's marvelous. It's just going to get better and better!

FURTHER READING

The Complete Wimmen's Comix edited by Trina Robbins (Fantagraphics, 2016)

Pretty In Ink: North American Women Cartoonists 1896–2013 by Trina Robbins (Fantagraphics, 2013)

Lily Renée, Escape Artist by Trina Robbins, Anne Timmons, and Mo Oh (Graphic Universe, 2011)

Excerpt from Gail Simone's *Batgirl* #19, revealing that Alysia Yeoh is transgender.

GAIL SIMONE
INTERVIEW • *Writer*

Like many women in contemporary comics, **Gail Simone got her start online.** But she wasn't making webcomics—she was calling out sexist tropes and misogyny in the medium she loved. Taking on the boys' club could have kept her from making comics, but her outspokenness had the opposite effect—soon she was writing for some of the superheroes she loved. Simone didn't leave her activism behind. Instead, she used the opportunity she was given to improve the representation of women and the diversity of characters in the medium.

Who are some of the creators that inspired you to write comics?

Being a comics fan from a small town even just a few years ago meant access to independent books, underground and Golden Age comics was extremely limited, so the number of working female comics creators I was exposed to was extremely small. I would latch onto any name that even seemed like it MIGHT belong to a female.

I bought almost every comic I could that had a woman in the credits. When I finally found a comics shop, it was almost overwhelming, books by Colleen Doran, Lea Hernandez, Wendy Pini, I just scooped them all up and really cherished them. And in superheroes, women like Louise Simonson and Devin Grayson were not just visible, but producing heartfelt, lovely work with *Superman* and *Batman*. I still glow a little bit when I think of them.

What was the industry like when you started working as a pro? How have you seen it evolve since then?

It was different, even a bit lonely at times. It's not that guys were unkind—most of my early support in both the professional and readership communities came from dudes. But it felt a bit solitary. If there were photos of pros working at DC, it would be thirty guys and me. If there was a panel at a con, five guys and me. It became a bit of a badge of honor, a point of pride, possibly as a survival mechanism, but also because I'm a farmer's daughter, and we tend to be stubborn. So, I stuck.

There was some crap thrown my way, there was and still is a lot of hate mail. But also, every day I wake up to lovely notes from people of all genders, people travel hours to conventions and appearances to come tell me that something I wrote meant something. I've always felt the readership was ahead of the publishers, they really just want great stories.

And it HAS gotten better. When I look at *The New York Times* bestselling graphic novel lists now, it's dominated by books that have a female presence on the creative team. The conventions have gender parity or very near, all over the world. And women are writing not just *Josie and the Pussycats*, but also *The Punisher*, which is a weird kind of progress, but progress nonetheless.

Your career started with "women in refrigerators," a phrase you coined to address the presence of female characters simply being a plot device to push the male characters' narratives forward. How did that shape your reputation, and the work you were offered?

Well, by all rights of logic, it should have wiped me from any consideration of working in comics. I have come to realize that that simple idea was a bit of a game-changer, a calling-out of the entire industry, and good LORD, the backlash was rough. I still get hate mail for it nearly constantly.

But a lot of pros understood what I was asking immediately, which was simply, "Why is this such a common trope? Why are these long-running female characters, that women relate to, being destroyed or de-powered as a catalyst for a male hero to go seek revenge?" And it hit, because it resonated.

I was just asking a question, but it made the national papers, there are articles about it to this day, and it became a bit of a monster. The phrase is used in all fiction now, it's used in Hollywood, it's used even in legal circles. And I've had people explain it to me, not knowing it was me who came up with the concept...

It's completely outgrown me. But I've always thought it was to the industry's credit that they took the hit, adjusted course a bit, and hired me regardless.

What I am proud of about the whole thing is, it made creators realize that women are reading their comics. I honestly think many had simply passed that possibility by.

You've been an incredible champion for women in the industry, particularly via social media. What has your experience been like, as a vocal, relentless feminist on the internet?

This is a bit sad, but when I started, a few of the women in comics seemed to actively resent, not me personally, but the idea of another woman taking up space in the industry. It was felt, I believe, that there was this tiny stretch of real estate that was marked WOMEN IN COMICS and someone new left less for them. That was kind of painful—I'd envisioned a sisterhood.

So, I really did vow never to be that person. I want to be the first person to welcome new women creators in, and the loudest to applaud when they succeed. Their triumphs don't threaten me, they inspire me. I think it's a lot healthier for everyone.

And I should also say that creators like Devin Grayson, Lea Hernandez and Colleen Doran were always encouraging. So, that helped tremendously.

There are always going to be people who hate you for being female. You might as well say what you truly believe and let them hate you for a good reason.

What advice do you have for up and coming creators who are facing sexism and gender politics in comics?

Just that it's serious. It's not trivial, and it's not something that should ever be waved away by saying, "It's getting better" or "I haven't experienced it personally." These tigers are behind the doors. I say, try to network, talk to other female creators, learn from their experiences. No one really does it all alone at this point, and they shouldn't have to.

But my biggest advice, both creatively and in terms of your career is simply this: be stubborn. If you know you're right, and you know your path, stick to your guns. There will be hurdles, there will be glue traps. You have to jump over them, and that can be difficult. But it's worth it.

What does the future of comics look like, and how do you think women will continue to change free expression in the medium?

We're here to stay, we're growing in number, and we're coming for your comics. It's too late to turn back, we're everywhere now, from the heads of publishing to the signing line at conventions. We're here, and we want the keys to the Batmobile.

FURTHER READING

Batgirl: The New 52 (multiple volumes) by Gail Simone and various (DC Comics)

Red Sonja (multiple volumes) by Gail Simone and various (Dynamite Entertainment)

Deadpool Classic, Vols. 9 and 10 by Gail Simone and various (Marvel Comics)

Noelle Stevenson's cover artwork for the inaugural issue of *Lumberjanes*.

(*Lumberjanes* #1, April 2014. Lumberjanes © and ™ Boom Entertainment Inc. Courtesy BOOM! Box.)

NOELLE STEVENSON
INTERVIEW • *Cartoonist*

At 24 years old, Noelle Stevenson has already had a hand in transforming comics for a new generation. From her webcomic-cum-National Book Award finalist *Nimona*, to her work on Eisner Award–winning *Lumberjanes*, to penning *The Runaways*, Stevenson has infused the industry with charming, relatable characters and expanded comics readership, especially among young women.

What was your early relationship with comics?

I grew up drawing a lot of comics, but I didn't know what they were at the time. Even before I could write, all I wanted to do was tell stories with my art. I'd dictate stories for my mom to write out for me, and then I'd illustrate them. As soon as I could write, I started making sequential art. Just stick figure sequences with vertical lines denoting "panels." Little stories about characters cleaning their houses, or the guy whose job it was to make traffic lights change color. I had a whole sketchbook that was just filled with the epic tale of an ant who rode roller coasters, and the roller coasters would crash, and he'd get maimed over and over. I didn't realize until much later that those were comics.

How have you seen the comics community change since you became a creator?

I feel like I've been in comics for 50 years, but it's been like, three. It's completely different now. Every year has been different from the last. I mean, three years ago we had the Hawkeye Initiative poking fun at the way female heroes were sexualized in comics art, and then last year there was a sexualized comic cover and it became a big deal, but it was a big deal because suddenly that wasn't the norm anymore. A lot has changed, but things tend to come in cycles—just with comics, that cycle is ridiculously fast. It's a lot to keep up with. I think there's a lot more change still to come. I hope there is.

When you started, how did you transition from fan art to webcomics?

Tumblr was at its peak at the time, and it was pretty easy to get art shared around there! So, by the time I went from fan art to an original webcomic, I had a pretty decent audience already. The transition from fan art to webcomics felt very natural, they felt very entwined for me. You have young creators taking the stories they love and making them the way they want to see them. I don't know what the art landscape on Tumblr is like these days—I haven't kept up with it—but webcomics remains the most exciting and promising comics form to me still. I think we're going to see a lot more exciting stuff coming from the webcomics crowd. I half want mainstream comics to pay more attention to them and half want them to be left alone because webcomics is evolving in such interesting and organic ways, and I don't think that they even need to be validated by major publishers. I want them to get paid, of course, but there are more options for that these days, too.

You've always made work that was very approachable for readers, regardless of gender. How do you think reading books like yours would have impacted you as a young person?

That's pretty much who I'm making them for! It feels like reaching backwards through time to give myself a pat on the back and say hey, kid, you're okay and there are a lot of other people like you. Practically, I'm hoping to reach those same types of kids today.

Freedom to read advocates have noted a disturbing trend: diverse comics are more likely to be censored. Why do you think that is, and how would

you respond?

People seem to be of the mind that kids can't handle something because they aren't familiar with it, and therefore it will be a big shock to them and they'll be scarred for life, or something. But really, whose fault is it that they aren't familiar with it? You trust your kid to be able to handle information about the world, and that's what will become normal for them.

What do you see as some of the risks to limiting access to diverse books, especially for readers who don't see an accurate portrayal of themselves in comics?

Right now, kids are growing up with a very narrow idea of who they're supposed to be because that's what's served

to them. It's our job to show them that those aren't the only ways to be. Normalize those narratives, let kids empathize with them, and give the ones who need it the most a mirror to see themselves in the story. Say, "Hey, this isn't a weird or bad way to be, this is just another way to exist in the world and it's great—you're great!"

What advice do you have for aspiring creators who feel restricted by perceptions of their gender and how they are "allowed" to connect with comics?

Don't wait for permission to create, and don't wait for approval on what you can create. Today more than ever, there are options for you to get your work out there exactly the way you want it without going through the old channels at all. Comics are being reinvented all around us constantly, and we need those new voices and new models more than ever.

How do you think the depiction and perception of gender will continue to change in comics in the future, both with regard to the creators of comics and with regard to the content?

I hope we reach a time in which female creators can make comics exactly the way they want to make them, and anyone who can't get on board gets left behind.

Excerpt from *Nimona*, Stevenson's National Book Award–nominated graphic novel.
(*Nimona*, p. 9. ©2015 Noelle Stevenson. Courtesy HarperCollins.)

FURTHER READING

Nimona by Noelle Stevenson (HarperTeen, 2015)

Lumberjanes (multiple volumes) by Grace Ellis, Noelle Stevenson, Shannon Watters, and Brooke Allen (BOOM! Box)

IN OTHER NEWS!!!

Katie Matthews' boyfriend, John Reddear, who goes to St. George's, dumped her. LE BIG DUMP! So this week Katie is wearing big black hearts on her hands. She draws them on with a sharpie in math class. Left one is nicer than right one. Similar problem as cast and photo.

It's kind of brutal watching someone walk around with broken hearts on their hands.

Mariko and Jillian Tamaki's *Skim* is based loosely on Mariko's experience in boarding school.

(From *Skim*, p. 11. ©2008 Mariko Tamaki and Jillian Tamaki. Courtesy Groundwood Books.)

MARIKO TAMAKI
INTERVIEW • *Writer*

Mariko Tamaki approaches making comics as though she and the artist are sitting outside the locked door to a room into which they want to see.

Her collaborations with her cousin Jillian Tamaki, *Skim* and *This One Summer*, have won numerous honors, with *Skim* being the first comic to receive a Governor General's Award nomination (in the text category) and *This One Summer* earning a spot on the shortlist for the Caldecott Medal, the first graphic novel to do so. We spoke with Mariko about defying conventions, challenging gatekeepers, and the future of comics.

What influences helped shaped your style of expression?

The Canadian literature I grew up reading in high school influenced me the most. I kind of nerdily declared when I was 15 that I would read every book Alice Munro, Margaret Atwood, Margaret Laurence, and Timothy Findley wrote. And I did for a few years (which you can imagine made me the most popular girl in school). There's something about Canadian literature, man. It puts you at this awkward but really interesting dinner party. And it's a REAL dinner party, where you can see the effort someone put into something, but you can also see the drippings burned into the side of the casserole dish and the orange neon price tag on the bottom of the candlestick. Canadian literature loves that stuff, and I do, too.

I'm also someone who spent a lot of time studying language in graduate school. The best part of grad school was finding out I loved talk, maybe even a tiny bit more than prose. I love how people tell a story with what they say, and that has definitely helped me with regards to writing in comics.

Finally, I think my biggest influence has been feminism, which is kind of like saying your biggest influence has been EARTH. Being a feminist was the reason I started to make art, first writing (bad) poetry in university, later making theater and writing essays when I moved back to Toronto. I've worked in feminist collectives writing songs and plays with six to eight other feminists. That's definitely a skill. It made me appreciate the joy of making something with someone other than myself. That said, I think feminism focused me in on the personal part of art-making. It made me want to make art for myself, to tell stories that were personal to me (though not necessarily about me), stories I cared about,

Mariko and Jillian Tamaki's *This One Summer* was the first graphic novel to be named a Caldecott Honor Book.

(Excerpt from *This One Summer*, pp. 90–91. ©2014 Jillian Tamaki and Mariko Tamaki. Courtesy First Second.)

which I think is a really important part of being an artist.

Beyond that my greatest influences have been the people I've worked with. Every time I make something with someone else, whether it's an editor or an illustrator, I realize something about how a medium works. I become better.

Your work has been attacked and challenged by censors. What was your reaction to the idea that your books are controversial?

It's a relatively relaxed thing, on a personal level, to be banned. I don't take it to heart at all. I think there are systems already in place inside libraries and homes, and inside readers themselves, that manage that sort of thing, so we don't have to pull books off the shelf.

I hear that there are people out there policing what they deem to be appropriate or inappropriate for young readers, but words like "appropriate" are so subjective. What's appropriate for young readers? Who do you picture these young readers to be? If you object to a book because it mentions someone being gay or shows two boys kissing, do you imagine all the people reading these books are straight?

I get that there are people who don't want their kid—or any kid—to read about violence or alcoholism or sex and sexuality. I want to write about the places where these issues connect with kids' lives. So we're at a stand-off. That's cool.

***This One Summer* was also named a Caldecott Honor Book. What was it like for you, having a book celebrated and criticized in the same breath?**

I generally feel celebrated and criticized all at once. That's like my life state. So, it was a familiar feeling.

Is there a point at which challenges and censorship can impact readers' abilities to see themselves authentically portrayed in stories?

If you pull a book from a library shelf, it's not available to the kid who gets their books at the library. So, you're impacting that library as a resource to the readers who depend on it. You also impact publishers who are making choices about what is a marketable book for young readers. So yes, you're definitely impacting the ability of a diversity of readers to connect with the books you deem inappropriate.

What are your hopes for the future of free expression in comics and how women in particular will continue to contribute to the medium?

I hope it just keeps getting freer. I love the mix of different perspectives I see coming into all parts of the comic book world. I'm super proud of the publishers that keep supporting interesting and diverse stories. I get a sense that we're moving forward. That diversity is important. That challenging the existing status quo and other people's conceptions of what a story for kids should be is important. I want more.

FURTHER READING

This One Summer by Jillian and Mariko Tamaki (First Second, 2014)

Skim by Mariko and Jillian Tamaki (Groundwood Books, 2008)

Raina Telgemeier's *Drama* explores friendship and crushes prompted by a school play.

(Excerpt from *Drama*, p. 192. ©2012 Raina Telgemeier. Published by Graphix, an imprint of Scholastic Inc.)

RAINA TELGEMEIER

INTERVIEW • *Cartoonist*

Not only has Raina Telgemeier created some of the most beloved comics of all time with *Smile*, *Drama*, and *Sisters*, she's won multiple Eisner Awards, an Ignatz Award, and a Boston Globe-Horn Book Award in the process. Even though people have been making intensely personal autobiographical comics for decades, no one has aimed their stories at young readers the way Telgemeier has. Her work is emotional and honest, and Telgemeier's ability to connect with her audience, reflected in her warm, expressive comics, isn't just changing the industry of today: it's inspiring the creators of the future.

You are absolutely one of the creators who has changed the landscape of comics. What are some comics that changed you as a creator?

Lynn Johnston's *For Better or For Worse* was the one that shaped me in my early days. Lynda Barry's *Ernie Pook's Comeek* was my YA, before YA existed. Ellen Forney's *Monkey Food: I Was Seven in '75* was a revelation. The works of so many other women have changed me: Ariel Schrag, Jessica Abel, Faith Erin Hicks, Liz Prince, Cece Bell, Kate Beaton, Svetlana Chmakova... the list goes on. The past and the present start to overlap.

You spend a lot of time directly interacting with young fans who will likely be the next generation of creators. What are you seeing from your fans that's different from your early experiences with comics?

Young readers have so much to choose from now. Between manga, webcomics, Big Two series aimed at kids, advances in e-reader technology, and the graphic novel boom in the bookstore and library markets, comics are in a great place for readers of every level to find an entry point. I didn't set foot in a comic book shop until I was 20, and before that, I got all of my comics in the newspaper or the humor section of bookstores. These days, you can walk into Target or Costco

and find amazing comics to read.

Your work has forged new possibilities for other creators and attracted readers to comics who otherwise might not have discovered the medium. How do you approach storytelling for these audiences?

I write for myself first. I follow my ideas down rabbit holes and see where they lead. Working with Scholastic has really sharpened my kid-sensibilities, and I talk over my various ideas with my agent and editor before anything makes it to the stage of pitching a project. They're tapped into the market and the forecast of children's literature, too. But my ideas usually start from somewhere

A chaste kiss between two male characters resulted in attempts to ban *Drama*.

(Excerpt from *Drama*, p. 188. ©2012 Raina Telgemeier Published by Graphix, an imprint of Scholastic Inc.)

deep inside, and that's frequently a potent memory from my youth.

Your book *Ghosts* is a pretty new direction for you, combining supernatural elements and heavier themes, like illness and death. Was there a sense of risk in journeying to a thematically darker place?

Honestly, I think I go to some pretty dark places in my nonfiction work, too! I approach fiction and autobio in pretty much the same way: starting with an emotional chord or image that really resonates with me, and building from there. No matter the genre, it's got to feel personal to me. It's always a little scary to try something that's unlike what came before, but I want to keep pushing myself to try new things and tell different kinds of stories as I grow as a creator.

You've experienced challenges to your work, most notably *Drama*, which features gay characters. CBLDF has noticed a trend that diverse comics are much more likely to face challenges. Why do you think that happens?

It's an old mentality. We still have gatekeepers from previous generations who feel they know what's best for their children and students and patrons. In many cases, this is true, but I think each reader needs to be considered on an individual basis.

What kinds of conversations do you have with your readers about the challenged material? How are you seeing them respond?

I discuss the characters in *Drama* as honestly as I discuss my other work. When I'm onstage in front of an audience, I don't filter. I don't soften my language. I say, "These characters are gay! They're based on some of my best friends!" There are six- and seven-year-old readers with their parents in the audience every time, and they all smile and nod their heads when I say that. Often, afterwards, a kid will approach me individually to thank me, or a parent will share an anecdote. I get a lot of amazing email, too. I don't read Goodreads or Amazon comments anymore, so most of the response I get is positive.

What do you see as the risks of diversity being targeted?

It sends a problematic message to readers. Every flavor of young person deserves to see themselves in literature, and the powers-that-be challenging content that isn't straight–white–cis–conservative tells everyone else that they're not worthy. The future is bright, though. The storytellers coming of age now have access to such a goldmine of diverse content, and they're already busy adding their own voices to the mix. I don't think anyone will be able to stop them.

FURTHER READING

Smile by Raina Telgemeier (Graphix, 2010)

Drama by Raina Telgemeier (Graphix, 2012)

Sisters by Raina Telgemeier (Graphix, 2014)

Ghosts by Raina Telgemeier (Graphix, 2016)

The Baby-Sitters Club (multiple volumes) adapted by Raina Telgemeier (Graphix)

Detail from the cover to the 2014 edition of the *Smut Peddler* anthology, co-edited by Trotman.

(Artwork by Jenna Salume. ©2014 Charlie Spike Trotman. Courtesy C. Spike Trotman.)

C. SPIKE TROTMAN

INTERVIEW • *Cartoonist & Editor*

Spike Trotman has redefined what it means to be an independent comics superstar. With her business acumen and financial savvy, her publishing company Iron Circus Comics has given a platform to new talent and underrepresented voices, while establishing a commitment to producing high-quality diverse content.

You're committed to ensuring underrepresented voices—women of color, queer people, people of lesser economic standing—are lifted up. What was the climate like in the comics industry when you began working toward telling these stories?

When I was getting started in comics, around the turn of the century, the scene was so different. Webcomics were new, untested, and widely distrusted as a legitimate medium. Old pros openly bagged on us. One prominent editorial cartoonist outright demanded to see tax returns from web cartoonists who claimed to make a living off their work. There were epic message board fights, mud-slinging, a lot of stuff I now recognize as old, established men frightened and angry that they might have to trade in their venerable status as syndicated cartoonists and go back to the bottom of the ladder. They were outright telling us we weren't just ruining our own careers, but theirs.

In hindsight, they were such ridiculous arguments. I didn't want to make newspaper comics or superhero comics, which were basically the two "serious" cartooning choices back then. I didn't pine to be part of the syndication system, or the assembly line system. Most of us making webcomics didn't. But every argument against them I heard hinged on the assumption we'd somehow flunked out of the two acceptable schools of pro comics and were out for revenge, torpedoing the careers of our betters. It sounds so bizarre now, but that's really how it was.

CBLDF has noticed an upsetting trend: diverse comics are more likely to be censored. Why do you think that happens? And how do you respond to these censors?

Comics have been traditionally singled out for suppression and censorship because of presuppositions they're children's fare, which is amazingly antiquat-ed. I'd argue American comics are only in the last decade or so finally becoming kid-friendly AGAIN, after decades of ignoring everyone except middle-aged white men.

I see a lot of the resistance against stories that diverge from the accepted comics "norm," be it a black Spider-Man or an autobiographical story about growing up in a funeral home, as reactionary. There's an element of society that thinks it owns comics. Any visible participation in comics by people unlike them, telling stories that aren't about them, don't even THINK of them? That's trespassing. So sometimes, attempts at suppression and censorship are just attempts at "course correction." They're the thoughts of people so accustomed to being catered to, accommodated and put first that the possibility something in their favorite medium did NOT prioritize THEIR attention and comfort is abomination.

I don't respond to attempts to stop me. Not only does my work not prioritize that segment of comics readership, I don't, either. They're a non-factor.

You're passionate about paying fair wages to your creators. Have you noticed stronger financial incentives for creators who prefer to work in mainstream comics instead of pushing for more visibility and diversity?

I don't notice much in "mainstream" comics at all. I know it's out there, but it's alien to what I do and what I'm interested in. For what it's worth, I sure would appreciate it if "diversity" meant more than palette-swapping a character here and there, or white, straight, cis guys trying to write more non-white, non-straight, non-cis characters. Comics can pat itself on the back about diversity when there are more marginalized people behind the scenes as well as on the page.

One of your most well-known projects is *Smut Peddler*, porn comics made by and for women. Were you ever afraid of censorship?

Honestly? No. It didn't ever occur to me I'd be censored, not in any way that mattered. The closest I've come to being censored is when a salty *Smut Peddler* rejectee reported the book's PDF sales to Gumroad, a service I used at the time, and had *Smut Peddler* kicked off the site. But that was about his envy, not trumped-up moral outrage. And I made some damn good lemonade down the line when I opened up a private store site. Damn good.

What do you see as the value in creating erotic comics?

There's nothing new about erotic comics. People have been making dirty drawings since we could scratch them on cave walls. What *Smut Peddler* brings to the table is sex-positive erotica that's about mutual pleasure and consent, where readers wouldn't be ambushed by non-consensual scenarios or misogyny or have to sit through angles and panels formulated exclusively for the heterosexual male gaze. *Smut Peddler* has been, literally, some readers' first inkling that it doesn't have to be that way. That's the biggest reward.

How do you see indie publishing changing the industry? What is your advice to anyone who wants to make comics outside of the big houses?

Indie and small press is the vanguard. Always has been. Large organizations are risk-averse and care deeply about the lowest common denominator; the indies don't have those worries. They can experiment, challenge their readers, try new things.

My only advice for someone who wants to make comics outside "the mainstream" is don't be afraid to make that comic they tell you won't sell, the comic you want to make. You're not some billion-dollar Disney subsidiary; you can afford to fail. And trust me, you will. Learn from your screw-ups and keep moving.

How do you think comics will change as more underrepresented demographics become involved?

Not just more diverse stories, but better-told ones that ring truer, from artists and writers who have been hungry to see people like themselves on the page for years. And not just the same color, gender identity or sexuality, but with more complex worldviews and experiences and sensitivities. People who are allowed to be characters instead of representatives or metaphors or something to motivate another character.

FURTHER READING

Templar, Arizona (multiple volumes) by C. Spike Trotman (Iron Circus Comics)

Poorcraft: The Funnybook Fundamentals of Living Well on Less by C. Spike Trotman and Diana Nock (Iron Circus Comics, 2016)

Smut Peddler (two volumes) by various (Iron Circus Comics, 2014 & 2016)

Wilson writes the current *Ms. Marvel* series, which features the first Muslim-American superhero.

G. WILLOW WILSON

INTERVIEW • *Writer*

After spending her early 20s in Egypt reporting on turbulent changes at the end of the Mubarak regime, G. Willow Wilson turned her pen towards fiction.

She developed broadly-acclaimed comics and the World Fantasy Award–winning novel *Alif the Unseen*. She is in the midst of writing what may be her most influential creation: Kamala Khan, a.k.a. Ms. Marvel, the first Muslim-American superhero, who has become a symbol of hope in the face of prejudice.

Could you describe your early experiences as a comics fan, and what the industry climate was like when you began your writing career?

When I first started reading comics, at around age 10, it was all about the books and the cartoons. I discovered the community that went with those things in my late teens. At that point, in the late '90s and early '00s, in the days of old-school internet message boards, it felt like a boys' club. To a certain extent, that feeling carried over into the industry itself, but there were some incredible women editors at the Big Two who had a lot of clout and weren't afraid to throw their weight around, so that mitigated things somewhat.

Which female professionals inspired and helped shape the direction of your work?

I would not have a career today were it not for DC editors Karen Berger and Joan Hilty, who championed my work early on. Having a Muslim writer floating around was not great optics for a comic book publisher. Every time I announced a new project, there would be a certain amount of blowback from right wing bloggers accusing me of being part of the Islamist socialist homosexual jihad on American values or whatever. I had zero pull in the industry at that point, and I was frankly afraid I was going to lose my job if the Islamophobes got loud enough and angry enough. But Joan and Karen—and Paul Levitz, who was president and publisher at DC at that point, and who I really adore—were totally unfazed. They encouraged me to push the envelope. So I did. You need an energy-filled, distraction-free environment to find your voice, and they gave me that environment. I will always be grateful to them for that.

Let's talk about Kamala Khan. She has helped lead the industry back to its rich tradition of teenage superheroes. Why do teenagers fit so well with the superhero story?

Being a teenager is all about figuring out who you are on your own terms. You're slowly decoupling from your family, developing your own ideas and tastes and goals. And at the same time, you're physically changing, growing into your adult body. That's a LOT to deal with at once. So it makes sense that the superhero origin story, which is often about suddenly discovering you are not who you thought you were, physically or emotionally, resonates powerfully with that archetypal coming-of-age narrative. When you get right down to it, a superhero origin story is really just a coming-of-age story with turbo-boosters.

Readers get a view into the lives and lifestyles of modern American Muslims through Kamala's family. Why is it important to make her home life such a big part of the book?

There's nothing worse than peopling a comic book series with supporting characters who are only there to walk on to the page, dispense cryptic wisdom, die in order to move the story forward, and then walk off again. I gave myself a rule: I had to know enough about each major supporting character to write a three-issue story arc from his or her point of view, if necessary. A superhero doesn't exist in a vacuum. They are shaped by the communities they serve. I think that is

Panel from Wilson's first graphic novel, *Cairo*.

(Published by Vertigo. Artwork by M.K. Perker. ©2007 G. Willow Wilson and M.K. Perker. Courtesy DC Comics.)

doubly true for a young, untested character like Kamala. So her community, and her family in particular, had to be very central.

CBLDF has seen a number of attempts to ban comics such as *Persepolis* and some children's books due to Islamophobia. How would you respond to this type of censorship?

I mop up my tears with royalty checks. Honestly, I don't know why anybody bothers to try to censor books anymore. Haven't they learned? Attempting to censor books sends sales through the roof. When you tell people a book is too risqué or dangerous to read, they will go out of their way to read that book, because now it has the appeal of something forbidden. You can't contain a story once it's out there.

What concerns did you have releasing Kamala into a culture in which hate against Muslims is so prevalent?

I thought Marvel would have to hire an intern just to open all the hate mail, but the tidal wave of hatred I expected never happened. Instead, Kamala quickly became a symbol of unity. She's graffitied on racist bus ads. Whenever something terrible happens, her "save one person, save all of mankind" meme resurfaces online. She's taken on a life of her own. It's been life-changing to watch.

Kamala is a standout example of recent diversity initiatives in comics. What are companies getting right? What progress still needs to be made?

Publishers everywhere have seen the writing on the wall. They know the audience is changing rapidly, and they can either adapt or face obsolescence. The old industry math, which says books led by women or minorities are doomed to fail, is becoming obsolete. The decision-makers—the editors, the publicists—have as important a role to play in shaping the future of the industry as creators and fans do. My great hope is that we will see more diversity not only in the books themselves, but also in the writers' room and on the editorial masthead.

FURTHER READING

***Ms. Marvel* (multiple volumes)** by G. Willow Wilson and various (Marvel Comics)

Cairo by G. Willow Wilson and M.K. Perker (Vertigo, 2007)

***Air* (multiple volumes)** by G. Willow Wilson and M.K. Perker (Vertigo)

For longer interviews, references, image bibliography, teaching guides, and other resources in support of *She Changed Comics*, please visit http://cbldf.org/she-changed-comics/

ADDITIONAL READING

ABOUET, MARGUERITE
Aya: Life in Yop City (Drawn & Quarterly)
Aya: Love in Yop City (Drawn & Quarterly)

ALLRED, LAURA
Madman (Image Comics)
iZombie (Vertigo / DC Comics)

ARAKAWA, HIROMU
Fullmetal Alchemist (VIZ Media)
The Heroic Legend of Arslan (Kodansha
    Comics)

BENNETT, ANINA
Boilerplate: History's Mechanical Marvel
    (Abrams Image)
Frank Reade : Adventures in the Age of Invention
    (Abrams Image)
Heartbreakers (Dark Horse Comics / Image
    Comics)

BRADDOCK, PAIGE
Jane's World (Bold Strokes Books)
Stinky Cecil (Andrews McMeel Publishing)

BRIGMAN, JUNE
Brenda Starr (syndicated, 1995–2011)
Power Pack (Marvel Comics)

CARROLL, EMILY
The Hole the Fox Did Make (webcomic)
Through the Woods (Margaret K. McElderry
    Books)

CLOONAN, BECKY
American Virgin (DC Comics)
Demo (Dark Horse Comics)
Gotham Academy (DC Comics)
Killjoys (Dark Horse Comics)
Southern Cross (Image Comics)

COLLINS, NANCY A.
Swamp Thing (Vertigo, 1991–1993)

Vampirella (Dynamite, 2014–2015)

CONNER, AMANDA
Harley Quinn (DC Comics)
Power Girl (DC Comics)
The Pro (Image Comics)

COOVER, COLLEEN
Bandette (Dark Horse Comics)
Gingerbread Girl (Top Shelf Productions)
Small Favors (Eros Comix)

CRUMB, SOPHIE
Sophie Crumb: Evolution of a Crazy Artist (W.W.
    Norton & Company)

DIMASSA, DIANE
Hothead Paisan: Homicidal Lesbian Terrorist
    (Cleis Press)

FLEENER, MARY
The Complete Wimmen's Comix (Fantagraphics)
Life of the Party (Fantagraphics)

FOGLIO, KAJA
Girl Genius (Night Shade Books)

GRAYSON, DEVIN
Gotham Knights
Nightwing (DC Comics, 2011–2006)
Catwoman (DC Comics, 1998–1999)
The Titans (DC Comics, 1999–2000)

GUERRA, PIA
Y: The Last Man (Vertigo / DC Comics)

HALL, BARBARA
Black Cat (Harvey Comics)
Blonde Bomber (Harvey Comics)
Girl Commandos (Harvey Comics)

HERNANDEZ, LEA
The Garlicks (webcomic)

Killer Princesses (Oni Press)
Teen Titans Go! (DC Comics)

HICKS, FAITH ERIN
The Adventures of Superhero Girl (Dark Horse Comics)
Brain Camp (First Second)
Friends with Boys (First Second)
The Last of Us (Dark Horse Comics)
The Nameless City (First Second)
Nothing Can Possibly Go Wrong (First Second)

HOEST, BUNNY
The Lockhorns (syndicated)

HOLM, JENNIFER L.
Babymouse (Random House)
My First Comics: I'm Grumpy (Random House)
My First Comics: I'm Sunny! (Random House)
Squish (Random House)
Sunny Side Up (Graphix)

IMMONEN, KATHRYN
Moving Pictures (Top Shelf Productions)
Never as Bad as You Think (webcomic)
Runaways (Marvel Comics)
Russian Olive To Red King (AdHouse Books)

JOHNSTON, LYNN
For Better or For Worse (syndicated)

KIERNAN, CAITLIN R.
The Dreaming (Vertigo / DC Comics)
The Girl Who Would Be Death (Vertigo / DC Comics)

KNISLEY, LUCY
An Age of License (Fantagraphics)
Displacement (Fantagraphics)
French Milk (Touchstone / Simon & Schuster)
Relish (First Second)
Something New (First Second)

LARSON, HOPE
Compass South (Farrar, Straus and Giroux)
Chiggers (Atheneum Books)
Goldie Vance (BOOM! Box)
Gray Horses (Oni Press)
Mercury (Atheneum Books)
Salamander Dream (AdHouse Books)
Who Is AC? (Atheneum Books)

A Wrinkle in Time (Square Fish)

LIU, MARJORIE
Dark Wolverine (Marvel Comics)
Monstress (Image Comics)
NYX (Marvel Comics)
X-23 (Marvel Comics)

MCNEIL, CARLA SPEED
Finder (Dark Horse Comics)
No Mercy (Image Comics)

POLLACK, RACHEL
Doom Patrol (Vertigo)

PRINCE, LIZ
Tomboy (Zest Books)
Will You Still Love Me If I Wet the Bed? (Top Shelf Productions)

RENÉE, LILY
The Werewolf Hunter (Fiction House)
Jane Martin (Fiction House)
Senorita Rio (Fiction House)

SWAIN, CAROL
Crossing the Empty Quarter and Other Stories (Dark Horse Comics)
Foodboy (Fantagraphics)
Gast (Fantagraphics)
Giraffes in My Hair: A Rock 'N' Roll Life (Fantagraphics)
Invasion of the Mind Sappers (Fantagraphics)

TAKEUCHI, NAOKO
Sailor Moon (Kodansha Comics)

TARR, BABS
Batgirl (DC Comics)
Motor Crush (Image Comics)

TYLER, CAROL
The Complete Wimmen's Comix (Fantagraphics)
Late Bloomer (Fantagraphics)
You'll Never Know Book 1: A Good and Decent Man (Fantagraphics)
You'll Never Know Book 2: Collateral Damage (Fantagraphics)
Soldier's Heart: The Campaign to Understand My WWII Veteran Father: A Daughter's Memoir (Fantagraphics)

INDEX

CONTRIBUTORS

CBLDF would like to thank the following people for their generous support of the Kickstarter campaign for *She Changed Comics*. You helped make this book a reality!

@novarants
@thoughtfulrat
A. David Lewis
A. Freeman
A. Hotte
A. Leigh Waldrop
Aaron Luk
Abby Walsh
Abigail Gordon
Acacia O'Connor
Adam Casey
Adam Debany
Adam J. Luna
Adam Jenkins
Adam Oelsner
Adam Richards
Adam Swift
Adam Wyman
Adrian Leverkuhn
Akasha Tsang
Alan G Morton
Alex and Kathy Johnson
Alex Barsk
Alex Fitch
Alex Grecian
Alex Hammond
Alex J
Alex Martin
Alexandra Craven
Alexandrea Kelly
Alexi Wheeler
Ali Grotkowski
Ali T. Kokmen
Alicia Duffy
Alicia Holston
Alisha Jade
Alison Cole
Alison Patten
Allstair Wallis
Allen Leung
Allison Blades
Allison O'Toole
Allison Radke-Bogen
Ally Shwed
Allyson Bright
Aloysius Beerheart

Alternate Reality Comics
alxd
Alyssa Leibow
Ama de Jong
Amanda Carroll
Amanda Clare Lees
Amanda Floyd
Amanda Jacobs Foust
Amanda Lea Green
Amanda O'Mara
Amanda Pate
Amanda Powter
Amber Kaill
Amber R. Perry
Amie DD
Amy Dallen
Amy L. Katz
André Katkov
Andrea Finuccio
Andrea Horbinski
Andrea Lundy
Andrew Belding
Andrew Thaxton
Andrew Wilson
Andy Haigh @Wolverinesclaws
Andy Shuping
angela d green
Angelina Conti
Angie Blackmon
Anita Kellams
Anja Komatar
Ann C.
Ann Myers
Ann Wells
Anna C. Mulch
Anna Warren Cebrian
AnnaMaria Jackson-Phelps
Anne Price
Anne Shelton
annemathematics
Annie Stinson
Annika Quint
Annika Samuelsson
Anonymous
Anonymous Adie

Antha Ann Adkins
Anthony C Mackaronis
Anthony C. Bleach
Aoi
Arcadian Comics & Games
Ariadna Molinari
Arianna Warner
Arianne Hartsell-Gundy
Arie Jane
Ariel Koh
Ariel Rosenfeld
Armond Netherly
Artemis Panagopoulos
Arya, Jennie & Alex Johnson
Ash Brown
Ash Static
Ashkan Abousaeedi
Ashlee Nelson
Ashley Cabico
Ashley Cabico
Ashley H.
Ashley Jo Thompson
Astarle
astrimage FILM
Aubrey Meeks
Aubrey S. DesPortes, Jr.
Audrey Redpath
Austin Hamblin
Avery Kim
Avri Klemer
Ayanni C. Hanna
B. Yeazell
B.A.'s COMICS
badfaery
Baker County Library District
Barbara Randall Kesel
Basia Kośla
Bea Witzel
Beatrix Abenathy
Beatriz C Bejarano
Becca
Becky Conzett
Becky Lutz
beckymmoe

Ben Koca
Ben Oxley
Benjamin Russell
Bess Holland
Bess Samuel
Bet Stett
Beth Rimmels
Bill Emerson
Bill Kohn
Bill Upham
Birte Lilienthal
Blair Mueller
Blythe Baldwin
Bob Halloran
Bob Keefer
Bob Lai
Bobby Derie
Bonnie N. Pollack, Ph.D.
Boobs Ruddock
Brad Brooks
Brad Kesler
Brenda Sohn
Brendan McGinley
Brenna Burwash
Brenton Cooney
Breta Moore
Brett Schenker
Brian Bram
Brian Gardes
Brian McKinley
Brian Rinkoski & Eliana Lane
Brian Sikkenga
Brian Weis
Britni Crankshaw
Brooke Hendrickson
Brookie Judge
Bruce A. Ritzen
Bruce Crossman
Bruno Boutot
Bryce Holland
Bunmi Oloruntoba
Byron H. Cuddeback
C J French
C.Medalis
Caela Mendini
caith_bpal

Caitlin Bridges
Caitlin Cedfeldt
Caitlin McEleney
Caitlin McGuren
Caitlin Rosberg
Callum Roper
Cam Collins
Cameron Petti
Camille
Candi Norwood
Cara B. Stone
Cara Bean
Caramellos
Caris Pelusey
Carissa Brunick
Carl Rigney
Carla H.
Carla Riemer
Carla Williams
Carlos Terra
Carly Burks
Carly Moniz
Carmen Johns
Carol L Tilley
Carol Mertz
Carole Giran
Carrie "Clips" McClain
Carrie and Jason Larsen
Caryn E. Neumann
Casey Cherry
Casper Neistrup
Cassandra Malo
Cassandra Pelham
Cassie Elle
Cat Mihos
Catherine Little
Catherine Noke
Catherine Temma
   Davidson
Cathy Brown
Cathy Green
Chad A. Burdette
Chadwick Ellis Boykin,
   Esq.
Chapter One Book Group
Charles "Meerkat"
   Cooper
Charles Hatfield
Charles P. Rhoads
Charlotte A. Churchill
Chas Lobdell
Chas! Pangburn
Chelle Marshall
Chelsea Cota
Chelsea Stone
Cheryl DF09
Chip Mosher

Chris & Maureen Mackar
Chris (CP) Powell
Chris Anderson
Chris Nine
Chris Rodriguez
Chris Simonds
Chris Sinderson
Chris Wilkes
Chrisann King
Christa J Seeley
Christian A Steed
Christian Albrecht
Christie Yant
Christina Laage
Christina Lorraine
   Harrington
Christina Vasilevski
Christine Gamble
Christine Zuba
Christo van Wyk
Christopher Gomis
Christopher Michael
   "Mykll" Valiant
Christopher Northern
Cici
Cindy C.
Claas Jaeger
Claire O'Brien
Claire Roe
Clare Nolan
Claude Weaver III
Claudia Berger
Claudia Miller
Clinton Diehl
Coffeeandgames
Colette Acheson
Colette Drouillard, PhD
Colleen Sullivan
Comic Art Factory
Comic Heaven
Comic Nurse
Comics Adventure
Constantine Markopoulos
Corey W. Taylor
Corinna Cornett
Corrie Allegro
Cosima Salim
Courtney Nguyen
Cristina Caballero
Crossover Comics
Crystal Sutherland
Cydney Ferguson-Brey
Cynthia Gonsalves
D Muir
D*H
D.M. Higgins

Dagmar Boer
Dan Hoizner
Dan Robb
Dan 'The Drizzle' Lewis
Dan Theodore
Dana Rae
Danella I Regis
Dani Leviss
Daniel Anderson
Daniel C Stillwaggon
Daniel Elkin
Daniel Kuester
Daniel L. Gillard
Daniel Meireles
Daniel Pierre Buhler
Daniel S. Lee
Daniel Schaefer
Daniel Taylor
Danielle & Adam Carey-
   Mooney
Danielle Indovino Cawley
Danielle Jolayne Robb
Danielle Lamoureux
Danilo B
Danny Barer
Danny Djeljosevic
Dara Parton
Dave Carter
Dave Forman
Dave Gray
Dave Herndon
   @NHDaveH
Dave Schrader
Dave Windett
Davery Bland
David A. Price
David Andry
David B. Rosengard
David Chaucer La Forest
David F. Pendrys
David Fitzgerald & Dana
   Fredsti
David Golbitz
David Harris
David James Miller
David Logvin
David McCarty
David Nissen
David S
David Saylor
David Steinberger
David Toccafondi
David Walls
Dawn Swain
DCBS
De André Nickens
Deal With It Comic - Tom

Deal
Dean Edney
Debbie Leung
Debby Weinstein
Deborah Malamud
Deborah Yerkes
Deena Jacobs
Denise Murray
depepi.com
Derek Royal
Derek Santiago
Diana Green
Diana Mallery
Diana Swartz
Diandra Mae
Diane Fox
dick rogers
Dictum Health
Dimetri & Adrienne Wilker
DL Warner
Dominic Quach
Don Leibold
donalfall
Donielle Gross
Donna Hutt Stapfer Bell
Donna Thompson
Donta M. Baker
Dorothy Mitchell
Doug Rednour
Dougie
Douglas Bushong
dougty
Dr Nick Gonzo
Dr. Johanna M.
   Broussard & Leigh
   Ward-Broussard
Dr. Joseph Willis
Dr. Lauren N. Woolsey
Drew Gilvary
Drew Kim
Drew Schneider
Dustin Alexander
E. Owens
E.D.E. Bell
Early Bird Studios
Ebonne
Echo Vents Books
Eddy Yue
Edel Cronin
Eduardo Cordova
Eduardo Daniel Toro
   Collazo
Edward Chik
Eileen Kaur Alden
Eileen Ramos
Eileen Urban
Eimi Okuno

El and Bryn Bryant-Walton
Elaine Tindill-Rohr
Elaine Wilson
Eleanor Smith
Elisabet Johansson
Elise Bowman
Elise M.
elizabeth
Elizabeth A. Janes
Elizabeth Brei
Elizabeth Sanders
Elizabeth Settoducato
Eljee Javier
Ellen Jane Keenan
Ellen Perry
Ellen Power
Elliott Sawyer
Emerson Lowrance
Emet Comics
Emily and Ann
Emily Garrison
Emily McCabe
Emily Sexton
Emily Thompson
Emily Vinci
Emma Levine
Emma Lord
Eric "djotaku" Mesa
Eric Hendrickson
Eric James Beasley
Eric Morgret
Erica Christianson
Erik L
Erika Altman
Erika J Turnbull
Erika Kramer
Erin Cavanaugh
Erin Hawley
Erin Kross
Erin Lynn Heath
Erin M. Hartshorn
Erin M. Wildman
Erin Subramanian
Esther Ellen Harrington
Ethan Daniels
Evan
Evan Miersch
Fabiana Boi
Faintdreams
Fanny Malovry
Fatima Iqbal
Fernando Del Bosque
Fi Stygall
Figie
Fiona C. Vajk Burgos

Fiona Morton (Fish)
Flo Ho
Florian Rubey
Florian Schiffmann
FoDeJo
Fran Haswell
Franchesca Vecchio Havas
Francine Lassen
Francisco Pinto
Frank Pitt
Fred Van Lente
Gail de Vos
Garima Agrawal
Gary Phillips
Gary Sassaman
Gary Simmons
Gashley Au
Gautham Kalva
Gavin Matthews
Gayle Francis Moffet
Gene Kannenberg, Jr.
Geoff Mochau
George Phelan
Gerd Ruprecht
Gina Curtice
Gladys Odegaard
Glenn G Amspaugh
Glennis LeBlanc
Globalsea
Glyn Williams
GMark Cole
Gord Godiva
Gordon Arata
Gordon McAlpin
Grace Confer-Hammond
Grace Waring
Graham McNicol
Greg "schmegs" Schwartz
Greg Coyle
Greg Griffin
GuiOhm
Guy Conn
Guy McLimore
Guy Thomas
Haley & Jessy Boros
Haley Williams
Hallie Jay Pope
Hana Anouk Nakamura
Hannah Duff
Hannah J. Rothman
Hanya Kim
Haviva Avirom
Hayley E Smith

Hazel Cashmore
Heather E. Pristash
Heather Faries
Heather Farrington
Heather McDaid
Heather Staradumsky
Heidi M. Wigler
Helen Ferguson
Helen Hammond
Helen Linda
Helena Runnels
Helene
Henry Pierpoint
Hermione Ramsay Speers
herpderpsoup
Hiljaisuus
Hillary and Natalie
Hillary Levi
Hobo613
Hollie Buchanan
Holly Aitchison
Holly Bemiss
Holly Monster
Holly Rowland
Hope Nicholson
Hub Comics
I. Fontaine
Iain S Ross
Ian O'Dea
Ilja P.
Immy Smith
Isabel C Martinez
Isabel Shaida
Isabella Vasquez
Isoline M. Sanderson
Iter Intergalactic
Ivan Salazar
J Babb
J Lily Corbie
J. A. Mäki
J. Kenneth Riviere
J.P. Polewczak
Jaap Tuinman
Jacine Passwaters
Jack Chiu
Jacklyn Hoffman
Jackson.R.Sullivan
Jacque Nodell
Jacquelynn Nguyen
Jade Higashi
Jadeduo
Jake Wilson
Jala Prendes
James Kennedy
James LaRue

James Lucas
James Marcucci
Jamie and Jonathan Gilmour
Jamie Ognibene
Jamie S. Rich
Jamie Susuras
Jamie Tanner
Jamie Vigliotti
Jamil Abdul kadiri
Jana Hoffmann
Jana Quintin
Jane Bancroft Cook Library
Janet Hetherington
Janice
Janice M. Eisen
Janice Tiburcio
Jannetje van Leeuwen
Jared at OK Comics
Jared Moore
Jasna Rodulfa Blemberg
Jason Abbott
Jason Best
jason e. bean
jason gessner
Jason Li
Jason Pasatta
Jason Penney
Jason Rudolf
Jason Sacks
Jay Lofstead
Jay Stern + M. Sweeney Lawless
Jeff Leeds
Jeff Lester
Jeff lowrey
Jeff Maza
Jeff Metzner
Jeff Miller
Jeff Pollet
Jeffrey Allan Boman
Jeffrey Edgington
Jeffrey K Hallock
Jeffrey Sanda
Jen Crothers
Jen M. Lott
Jen Scott
Jen Vaughn
Jenifer Redwood
Jenn
Jenn Wells
Jennevieve Schlemmer
Jenni Sands
jennifer and the beans
Jennifer Holm
Jennifer K Ryan

Jennifer K. Koons
Jennifer K. Stuller
Jennifer King
Jennifer L Porter
Jennifer Muzquiz
Jennifer Pawley
Jennifer Yi
Jeremy Fried
Jeremy Ladan
Jeremy Weinstein
Jeremy Wiggins
Jeska Kittenbrink
Jess Ray
Jesse Hardesty
Jesse Masterson
Jesse Morgan
Jessi Jordan
Jessica Bader
Jessica Boyd
Jessica Ikley
Jessica Jones
Jessica Leigh Clark-Bojin
Jessica Marie Getty
Jessica Prowant
Jill Chinchar
Jill DeLong
Jill Gensler
Jill Millar
Jill Thompson
Jilna Shukla
Jim Kosmicki
Jim M. Cripps
Jim McClain
Jo Turner
Joan Reilly
Joanna Turner
Joanne Elizabeth Stanley
Jocelyne Allen
Jody Broad
Joe Bettis
Joe Crawford
Joe Germuska
Joe Glass
Joe Sergi
Joe Stone
John Boreczky
John Chadwick
John D. Roberts
John Duncan
John Dupuis
John Kovalic
John Lustig
John M Gamble
John Maddening
John Merklinghaus
John Monahan

John Romero
John Romkey
Johnny Mayall
Joi Lakes
Jon Folkers
Jonas Eckerman
Jonas Lyngbek Thestrup
Jonathan "Munch" Keim
Jonathan McGaha
Jonathan Petersen
Jordyn Bonds
Josan
José Muñoz
Joseph Fernandes
Joseph Moseley
Josh Vann
Joshua Hale Fialkov
Joshua Tims
Joyce Ann Garcia
JP Carney
Judez Neidorff
Judith Bienvenu
Judith Collard
judy johnson
Jules Dowling
Julia Perilli
Julie Benson
Julie Blake
Julie Meridian
Julie Nick
Juliet McMullin
Jumpsaround
Junebug
Junelle Ward
Juniper Nichols
Juniper Sage
Justin Izbinski
Justin Pinner
Jyoti Alexander
K Parker
K. D. Bryan
K. Macdonald
k.d.prosser
Kaleigh Busch
Kami Sunde
Kara Captain Whizbang
    Swanson
Kara Marie Sheaffer
Karen Beilharz
Karen Exline
Karen Gillmore
Karen Green
Karen J Deeter
Karen Munk
Karen Sylvester
Karen Watt

Karl Almén Burman
Karla Hyde
Karon Flage
Kasra Ghanbari
Kat Kan
Kat Martine-McEvoy
Kate Baker
Kate Blake
Kate D.
Kate Ellingsen
Kate Ellis
Kate Feirtag
Kate Kloetty
Kate Kosturski
Kate Larking
Kate Nickle
katetruth
Katherine Malloy
Katherine S
Katherine Sibly
Kathleen McDowell
Kathleen Sweeney
Kathryn Hemmann
Kathy Flynn
Katie and Lauren Min
Katie Armentrout
Katie McDonough
Katie McGuire
Katie Morton
Katie Spear
Katie Turcotte
Katri Houtbeckers
Katrin Wheatley
Katrina Lehto
Katy Rex
Katy Schroeder
Katy Shunk
Katy Welte
Kay Maruhashi
Kayley Thomas
Kazoo magazine
Keith F.
Kelly Bahmer-Brouse
Kelly Doe
Kelly Lannon
Kelly Moravec
Kelly Phillips
Kelly Ziemski
Kelsey Avril
Kelsey R. Marquart
Kelson Vibber
Ken Myers
Ken Rokos
Kendra L
Kenneth Chisholm
Kenny Beecher

Keri Bas
Keri Oleniach
Kevin Cuffe
Kevin D. Bond
Kevin Donlan
Kevin Harrison
Kevin J. "Womzilla"
    Maroney
Kevin Kite
Kevin Maynes
Kevin McGoldrick
Kim Fisher
Kim Ku
Kim Lindberg
Kimberly M. Lowe
Kimberly Spencer
Kira Askaroff
Kirstien Kroeger
Kitty P.
Kiwi Carranza
KJ Weir
Kora Bongen
Kory C. & Dana I.
Kris McQuage-Loukas
Kristal J Feldt
Kristen Garcia
Kristen Simon
Kristi McDowell
Kristilyn
Kristin Ruhle
Kristina Cary
Kristina Handy
Kristine West
Kurt Hoss
Kyla Blythe-Prahl
Kyle Rose
L. Coller
L. Renee
L.R. Townes
Lacey Skorepa
Lady Demona
Lana Berman
Lance Anderson
Lang Thompson
LaRonika Thomas
Laura Clements
Laura Given
Laura Kittleson
Laura Light
Laura Quilter
Laura Stabler
Laura Woods
Laurel Jensen
Laurell Hamilton
Lauren Hanna
Lauren Hoffman

Lauren Roy
Laurence
Laurie A. MacDougall
Lea J. Zimmt
Leah Brown
Lee Bennett
Lee F Dickens
Lee Rusty Mothes
Lee-ann Dunton
Lemonssky
Lennhoff Family
Leo Milciades Sanchez
Leonardo Soledad
Leron Culbreath
Leslie S. Klinger
Levi Fleming
Liam Otten
Ligeia Minetta
Linda Simensky
Linden Couteret
Lindsay Vaiceliunas
Lindsey Knoll
Lindy
Lionel English
Lisa Bateman
Lisa Ferneau-Haynes
Lisa Lees
Lisa Martincik
Lisa Oldoski
Lisa Smith
Liz Colacino
Liz Enright
Liz K.
Liz Van Winkle
Lora Wagers
Lorenzo Luna
Lori Crawford
Lori Stewart
Lorna Stebbins Fossand
Lostwhilecaching
Louise R. Adam
Lu Wee Tang
Lucia CS
Luciana Rushing
Lucile Perkins-Wagel
Lucy Hancock
Lynn Rosskamp
M Dafni
M.M.S
Maaike van Eekelen
Mackenzie Grover
Mackenzie Wray Stone
Madalyn Simpson
Maddy Melnick
Madeleine Fenner
Madeleine Holly-Rosing

Madeleine Lloyd-Davies
Magdalena Olchawska
Maggie & Mike Moninski
Makayla LaRue
malpertuis
Mama Jane
Manu
Manu Gabaldón
Marc Ward
Marcela Peres
Marcia Rojas
Margaret Kunz
Margaret St. John
Margreet de Heer
Marguerite Dabaie
Mari Ahokoivu
Maria Alisa Santiago
Maria Cielo Ludwig
María Eugenia Reimunde
Maria Ey. Luihn
Marianna "Kisu"
    Leikomaa
Marianne McDonald
Marie-Anne
Marina Müller
Mario J. Sifuentez
Marion Valis
Marion Valis
Marisa Stotter
Marissa Stellwag
Maritza Sieders
Mark "3D" Kernes
Mark A. Parchman
Mark L. Van Name
Mark O'Brien
Mark S. Weller
Mark Verheiden
Mark Wright
Marlena D. Astorga
Marmæl
Marni Stanley
Marni Stanley
Martin Andersen
Martin M. Hernandez, Jr.
Martin stenkilde
Marty Lloyd
Marvin Miller
Mary Kathryn Hammond
Mary Todd
Matilda Kirchen
Matt Downer
Matt Sanders
Matt W Haas
Matt Zitron
MatteoS
Matthew and Laura Krug

Matthew Becker
Matthew Bendert
Matthew Bitley
Matthew Kirshenblatt
Matthew N. Noe
Maura McHugh
Maureen Cunningham
Max & Carol Hime
May Liu
Maya
MC Brickell
Meagan Ellis
Meesi Calabresi
Meg Jones
Meg Lemke
Megan Bethke
Megan Byrd
Megan DeYarman
Megan Puebla
Megan Puga
Megan Thomas
Megan Walling
Meghan K. Callahan
Meghan Thompson
Melanie Creer
Melanie Nazelrod
Melinda Luisa de Jesus
Melissa Braeger
Melissa Bryan
Melissa Fortenbery
Melissa Tallman
Menachem Cohen
Meredith & Paul Reese
Meredith Yayanos
Mey Valdivia Rude
Meyer-Curley Family
Mia R. B.
Micaela "MJ" Godfrey
Michael Abbott
Michael Cathro
Michael Dalpe
Michael Dooley
Michael Groman
Michael J. Engel
Michael Lorenson
Michael Lovell
Michael Mazzacane
Michael Meltzer
Michael Scheuermann
Michail Dim.
    Drakomathioulakis
Michel Olivieri
Michele
Michelle Johnson
Michelle Porter
Michelle Reid

Michelle Stoliker
Michelle VanSetten
Michelle Y. Morris
Miguel "Paco" Alderete
Mikayla Hutchinson
Mike "ComicsDC" Rhode
Mike Beck
Mike Bundt
Mike Cassella
Mike Fitzpatrick
Mike Furth
Mike Lewis
Mike Losso
Mike Rende
Mike Shema
Mike Speakman
Milan Kovacs
Millie Forrester
Min Jung Kim
Mina Gaughran-Perez
Minzoku
Miranda Richardson
Mireille Roddier
Mirva Lukkari
MJ Jacob
Mock
Moira and Evelyn
Mollie E
Mollie Hall
Molly Black & Katreya
    Lovrenert
Monica A. Rocha
Monica West
Monika Kanokova
Morten Poulsen
Mudd Law Offices
Mx. Angela Pettengill
N Hatchman
N. C. Christopher Couch
Nancy Nowacek
Nangijala IF
Naomi Quinn
Nat Gertler
Natacha
Natalie Chenard
Natalie Freeman
Natalie Neal-Peters
Natalie Nolan
Nate Hartz
Nathalie Samson
Nathan Crawford
Nathan Herald
Nathan Kellen
Nathan Zoebl
Nathaniel Booth
Nathaniel Cafiero

Navin Bhambhani
Nedra Rezinas
Neil
Nesher G. Asner
Nic McPhee
Nicholas George
Nicholas J. McBurney
Nicholas Stylianou
Nick FitzHerbert
Nick Gonzales
Nick Guerrera
Nick Sousanis
Nicolaj Klitbo
Nicole & Neil Carver
Nicole Jeppsen
Nicole Solis
Nicole Trainor
Niki Carlson
Niki Pentland
Nikki Boisture
Nikki Hung
Nikki Zano
Nina Brottman
Niraj Patil
Noah Kuttler
Noah M. Benzion
Olivia Gray
Omar Ravenhurst
Ora McWilliams
Outsider Press
pablomoses
Paden Wyatt
Pål Ströbaek
Pam Steele
Pamela Forbes
Pang Peow Yeong & Family
Parker & Loïe Tran
Patricia Langevin
Patrick Holt
Patrick McEvoy
Patrick Mohlmann
Patrick Reitz
Patrick Ridings
Paul Barrera
Paul Daniel
Paul Fisher Davies
Paula Gaetos
Paula Hearn Chandler
Pearly Ong
Peggy Foster
Peggy J. Hailey
Peggy Twardowski
Pete Bielek
Peter Gerhardt
Peter Kenney

Peter Monks
Peter Strömberg
Peyton Eyre
Pharoah "Tatsujinedge" People
Phil Hester
Philip Maddox
Philip Pangrac
Phillip Koop
Pied Piper, Inc.
Pierre Charrel
Pini
Pippa Guzman
Poop Office
Qiana Whitted
R. Adam Moore
R. Sikoryak
Rachael Burford
Rachel "Nausicaa" Tougas
Rachel and Danny Shapira
Rachel Connor
Rachel Everett
Rachel Liell
Rachel Penniman and Bryan Andregg
Rachel Shippam
Rachelle Stein
Rae Grimm
Rae K
Rafael Maia
Rafer Roberts
Raina Telgemeier
Rajel Fridman
Ralph
Ram V
Randall Paske
Randall W. Barfield
Randi N Richards
Randy Wood
Ray Cornwall
Raymonde Bonin
RazéLatte
Rebecca Griffiths
Rebecca Henely
Rebecca Ng
Rebeka G.
Red Lhota
Regina Joskow
Rémi Gauthier
Rémi Gérard-Marchant
Rhiannon Raphael
Ricardo Gomez
Riccardo Sartori
Rich Johnston
Rich Radka

Richard Christpher
Richard Franklin & Aletha Basconcillo
Richard Gray
Richard Pini
Rigo Rich
Rita L. Warcholic
Rob Atwood
Robert Altomare
Robert Crichton
Robert Dahlen
Robert E. Stutts
Robert Gavla
Robert J. Guadagno
Robert Kass
Robert Kinosian
Robert Riley-Mercado
Robin Anderson
Robin Bayless
Robin Jeffrey
Robin L. Zebrowski
Robyn M.
Robyn Pearson
Rocío Sosa Marqués
Rocket !
Rodolfo Schmauk
Rom Rom
Ron Trembath
Ronell Whitaker
Ronnie Ball
Rory O'Connor
Russell B. Farr
Ruth Ann Harnisch
Ryan D Lucchesi
Ryan D. Beach
Ryan Dunlavey
Ryan French
Ryan McCulley
Ryan N. Olsen
S. Mickey Lin
Sabrina Degas Pont
SallyRose Robinson
Salvador Castro
Sam Coaass
Sam D.H.
Sam Klai
Sam Malone
Sam Neukirch
Sam Stander
Samantha Netzley
Sami Nikander
Sandrene Mathews
Sandy King Carpenter
Sandy Travis and Wayne Beamer
Sara C

Sarah
Sarah & Jean
Sarah Agterhuis
Sarah B. Ratner
Sarah Braun
Sarah E. H. Thomas
Sarah Gaydos
Sarah Haskins
Sarah Kate Merry
Sarah Laghribi
Sarah Livingston
Sarah M. Huth
Sarah Miller
Sarah Sax
Sarah Seifert
Sasha Spears
Satine Phoenix
Savonna Stender-Bond-esson
School of Visual Arts Library
Scott Almes
Scott Bradley
Scott Harriman
Scott Morrison
Scott Rowland
Scott Rubin
Sean Gaffney
Sean Lally
Sean McGinley
Sean Patrick McCarron
Sean Whelan
Sebina Christensen
SED Mitchell
Selena Knight
Selin Sonmez
Senna Alarid
Sergey Anikushin
Serpico Kids
Shane Alonso
Shane Davis
Shane Heckethorn
Shane Martin DeNota-Hoffman
Shanea Ehrensberger
Shannon Campbell
Shannon Hayes
Sharmini Markandu
Shaun J Cobble
Shawn Churchill
Shawn Cunningham
shayne avec i grec
Sheala
Sheilah Villari
Shelby Goicochea
Shell Graves
Shelley DeVost

Sherry LaBelle
Shervyn
Sheryl Stahl
Shield Bonnichsen
Shira Neiss
Shirley
Simon Fraser
Simon J Davies
Simon Pearce
SJ Aylett
Skybur
Slevin Kelevra
Society of Illustrators
Solène Leti
Soli-chan
Son Slaughter
Sonia
Sonnet Sakievich
ST
Stacey & Michelle Scrimgeour
Stacey Lindholm
Stacey Morin
Stacy Bias
Stacy Fluegge
Stasia Archibald
Stefan M. Manolov
Stefanie Ramirez
Stephanie
Stephanie Carey
Stephanie J. De La Torre
Stephanie Jobe
Stephanie Noell
Stephanie Santos
Stephanie Tarter
Stephen C. Ward
Stephen Kelley
Stephen R. Bissette
Stephen Wark
Sterling C Jones
Steve
Steve Sick
Steve Siwy
Steve W
Steven Castro
Steven Savage
Stone Robot Enterprises
Stories Bookshop + Storytelling Lab
Sue Lilly
Suki Valentine
Super Aarthi
Susan Bullock Sylvester
Susan E Wilson
Susan McCullough
Susan Munn

Susan Phillips
Susan Ruzicka
Susan Staton
Susan Tarrier
Suzanne Lau Gooey
T. Adam
T. Kok & S. Kay
T.D. England
Tabbs
Tabetha Frey
Tabetha Wallace
Tahirah Alexander Green
Talita "Setheus" Amaral
Tasha Doyea
Taso Mullen
Ted Adams
Ted and Trang Lai
Ted Hahn
Ted Wesley
Teme Ring
Teodoro Peralta
Teresa Danielle Lynch
Terri & Thomas Hodges
Terri Connor
Terrianne McGrath
Terry Ann Wright
The Cat Startler
The Fastiggi Family
The Fenstermakers
The Sequential Artists Workshop
Theo Clarke
Theresa Yera
Thomas Fayne
Thomas Lee Parker
Thomas the Martyr
Thomas Tremberger
Tiffany R Engle
Tim Meakins
Tim Nicholls Harrison
Tim Tjarks
Tim Vojta
Tina Az
Todd Coopee
Todd Good
Tomus Cone
Toni Shelton
Tony Heugh
Tracey Knouff
Travis Dunn
Tricia Lupien
Trip Space-Parasite
Trista & Daniel Robichaud
Tristan J. Tarwater
Tsuyoshi Kawahito
Tuesday Aucoin

Tyler Chin-Tanner
Vance Kotrla
Vanessa Hall
Vanessa Sanford
Vanja Utne
Velvet and Mud
Vera Zago
Verity Sathasivam
Verónica Muñiz-Soto
Veronica Ramshaw
Veronika Temml
Vicki Woodbury
Victoria Coberly
Victoria E.S. Pullen
Victoria Haddow
Victoria Stolfa
Vince Averello
Vincent Kukua
Vinicius Rodrigues Queiroz
Vinnie Penna
Virginia Partridge
Vivienne Jones
vjbseven
W. Evan Sheehan
W. Joey Thornton
Wally Hastings
Walter Holowatenko
Wanda Hamilton-Widrig
Ward McMillan
Warren Wannamaker
Warsaw Seidels
Wendy Walter
Wesla Weller
Wesley L.
Will K Dozier
William O. Tyler
William Yuya Mix
Win Bent
Xandra Coe
Yaika Sabat
Yvette Arteaga
Yvette Couser
Zachary Gilpin
Zack Kruse
Zelda Newhouse-Bailey
Zoe Grey Decena
Zoe Lewycky
Zoe Susannah Rosso

About the Comic Book Legal Defense Fund

Comic Book Legal Defense Fund is a non-profit organization protecting the freedom to read comics! Our work protects readers, creators, librarians, retailers, publishers, and educators who face the threat of censorship. We monitor legislation and challenge laws that would limit the First Amendment. We create resources that promote understanding of comics and the rights our community is guaranteed. Every day we publish news and information about censorship events as they happen. We are partners in the Kids' Right to Read Project and Banned Books Week. Our expert legal team is available at a moment's notice to respond to First Amendment emergencies. CBLDF is a lean organization that works hard to protect the rights on which our community depends. For the latest news and to access our full archive of resources, please visit **www.cbldf.org**

CBLDF does this work thanks to the support of our members. We have membership plans for donors in every budget, and all of them are tax-deductible!

Please support our important work by joining CBLDF today!
http://cbldf.myshopify.com/collections/memberships

2016 membership card artwork
by Craig Thompson (*Blankets,
Habibi, Space Dumplins*)